"ONE OF MY FAVORITE COOKBOO[...] SO-BEZ-221
DOWN-TO-EARTH, SIMPLIFIES AND DEMYSTIFIES THE BREAD-
MAKING PROCESS."

—Wethersfield Connecticut Post

The best-selling classic bread-baking book is back and it's better than ever, completely revised, updated, and expanded to give bakers over 100 easy, mouth-watering recipes—two thirds of them brand new.

Whether you're an accomplished baker who loved the original and wants more variety and new ideas or a beginner eager to learn, you'll find that these wonderful, completely tested recipes offer detailed yet simple, easy-to-follow instructions to fit any level of expertise. BAKE YOUR OWN BREAD is the breadbaker's best friend.

"An excellent book for beginners to use as a bible."

—Knoxville News Sentinel

"Offers countless ways to bake bread that not only tastes better but is better for you."

—The Sacramento Union

FLOSS and **STAN DWORKIN** are co-authors of *The Apartment Gardener* and *The Good Goodies*. A former radio/TV show team in New York City, they are also bread-baking instructors. Stan is the author of the *Jockey Club Cookbook*.

1. Swedish Saffron Wreath (page 112)
2. Rich Whole Wheat Bread (page 24)
3. 100% Whole Wheat Bread (page 26)
4. Italian Bread (page 38)
5. Pumpernickel (page 142)
6. Quick-Rising Whole Wheat Figure-Eight Squash Rolls (page 70)
7. Quick-Rising Cheese Braid (page 64)
8. Bran Drops (page 228)

BAKE YOUR OWN BREAD
Revised and Expanded

by

Floss and Stan Dworkin

Illustrations by
Floss Romm Dworkin

A PLUME BOOK

PLUME
Published by the Penguin Group
Penguin Books USA Inc., 375 Hudson Street, New York, New York 10014, U.S.A.
Penguin Books Ltd, 27 Wrights Lane, London W8 5TZ, England
Penguin Books Australia Ltd, Ringwood, Victoria, Australia
Penguin Books Canada Ltd, 2801 John Street, Markham,
Ontario, Canada
L3R 1B4
Penguin Books (N.Z.) Ltd, 182-190 Wairau Road, Auckland 10, New Zealand

Penguin Books Ltd, Registered Offices: Harmondsworth, Middlesex, England

Published by Plume, an imprint of New American Library, a division of Penguin
Books USA Inc.

BOOKS ARE AVAILABLE AT QUANTITY DISCOUNTS WHEN USED TO PROMOTE PRODUCTS
OR SERVICES, FOR INFORMATION PLEASE WRITE TO PREMIUM MARKETING DIVISION,
PENGUIN BOOKS USA INC., 375 HUDSON STREET, NEW YORK, NEW YORK 10014.

A hardcover edition was published by New American Library and simultaneously
in Canada by The New American Library of Canada Limited (now Penguin Books
Canada Limited).

This is a revised and expanded edition of *Bake Your Own Bread*, originally
published in hardcover by Henry Holt and Company, Inc. and in paperback as a
Signet book.

 REG.D TRADEMARK—MARCA REGISTRADA

Library of Congress Cataloging-in-Publication Data

Dworkin, Floss.
  Bake your own bread.

  Rev. ed. of: Bake your own bread and be healthier.
1st ed. © 1972.
Includes index.
  1. Bread. I. Dworkin, Stan. II. Dowrkin, Floss.
Bake your own bread and be healthier.   III. Title.
TX769.D96   1987   641.9′15   86-33135
ISBN 0-453-00553-5
ISBN 0-452-26464-2 (pbk.)

First Plume Printing, January, 1989

   5 6 7 8 9 10 11

PRINTED IN THE UNITED STATES OF AMERICA

To absent friends
Goodness, Ben, and Stella

Bread baking is a lot like married love.
The first loaves of bread you make are not
the best you'll ever make, but they're better
than any you've ever bought.

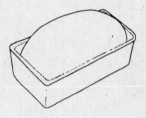

Contents

Introduction to the Revised and Expanded Edition

FIFTEEN years ago, when we began teaching bread baking in our big old kitchen, we looked for a text for our students to take home with them. It had to be a book that assumed no prior experience, and it actually had to teach bread baking. We couldn't find it—so we wrote it.

We wrote *Bake Your Own Bread* the way we taught the classes. Everyone started out kneading white breads, and then slowly we suggested nutritious substitutions and additions, and then we introduced them to whole wheat.

In this new edition, we have come out of the closet, and we show our true colors by starting out with what is *our* daily bread—whole wheat bread.

We have written this revised edition of *Bake Your Own Bread* because we found that we had lots more to say about breads—we had new ideas, new techniques, and we had developed many new recipes.*

In the original edition, we spent a lot of time explaining and justifying the nutritional and health advantages of baking your own bread. Fifteen years ago, only "nuts" ate nuts and whole grains. Now, millions of people eat complex carbohydrates and fiber for breakfast every morning.

Nowadays you can buy stone-ground whole wheat flours right off your supermarket shelf. You don't even have to know where to find a health food store.

---

* For those who think bread is necessarily fattening, all of these recipes were baked, tested, and tasted by Stan. In the six months of working on the revision, *he lost 55 pounds.*

We have kept all of the original recipes of *Bake Your Own Bread* in this edition, but they have been reworked for simplicity. The teaching has not been thrown out; it has just been put elsewhere. Most of our techniques and the major ingredients we use are found in Chapter 1. Tools and other terms are explained in the Glossary, near the end of the book. If you come across something in a recipe that you do not recognize or understand, check both places before you panic!

We have also added new recipes to explore areas of baking not included in the original edition: Quick-Rising Breads, Ethnic Breads, Muffins, Biscuits, Popovers—and much more.

About six years ago, we got a letter from a happy reader—one of hundreds of letters we've received about *Bake Your Own Bread*. The letter had taken five months to reach us because it had come from Easter Island in the South Pacific. The writer thanked us for the book, and told us how his health had improved, starting with the recipes in *Bake Your Own Bread*.

Thank *you*, Easter Island, and the hundreds of thousands of readers who read *Bake Your Own Bread* in the original edition. This revision is for you.

Introduction to the
First Edition:
Down with the Mystique

OVER the years a mystique has grown up around bread baking; a kind of mystery (in the old Greek sense of a secret religious society) which excluded the outsider who hadn't learned the rites at Mother's knee. Recently, however, there has been a renaissance of interest in home baking—probably a reaction to much of the artificiality in our food and a desire to eliminate some of the additives *they* keep sneaking into our lives. This interest in baking is part of the overall growth in interest in improving the quality of what goes into our stomachs.

This book is a "guide to the perplexed," to steer you through the simplicities of bread baking and through the complexities of improving your diet by baking your own bread.

It is not everything you ever wanted to know about baking but couldn't find out from your mother. Rather, it provides a foundation of techniques and recipes which, once mastered, will enable you to go on to virtually any bread, inventing recipes of your own, or adapting standard recipes to greater wholesomeness, improving your own and your family's health.

As for the mystique—there is none. Bread baking is a simple process, easily learned, quickly mastered by woman, man, or child, a satisfying and delicious pastime, a rewarding addition to everyday cooking, even profitable if you have the business sense.

BAKE
YOUR OWN
BREAD

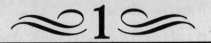

Techniques and Ingredients

THIS chapter introduces you to the major techniques and ingredients we use in this book. *And you don't need to read any of it to bake bread!* If you feel secure and brave, skip right to the recipes. If, however, you want the support of explanations of how and why and with what ingredients we bake, then this chapter is for you.

Definitions of unfamiliar terms can be found in the Glossary at the end of the book.

KNEADING

Many flours contain a protein substance called gluten which, when rubbed against itself, develops elasticity. This elasticity gives cohesiveness to dough, holding the bubbles formed by the yeast and allowing the dough to rise.

To develop the elasticity, you rub the particles of dough against one another by pushing and pressing the dough with your hands—a process called kneading.

Elasticity can be formed quickly by vigorous handling, or it can be formed slowly by gentle handling.

In the recipes we give kneading times. These are averages. If a recipe calls for 8 minutes of kneading, you can't tickle the dough

1

for 8 minutes and expect the elasticity to be developed. In the same way, if you come home angry and attack the dough like a samurai, you may get the elasticity developed in as little as 5 minutes. You *can* tickle the dough, but it may take you 20 minutes of tickling to get the elasticity happy enough to rise the bread.

Techniques of kneading are almost as varied as the people who knead. Some bakers like to squeeze and then slam the dough against the board. Some like to push, some like to press down. We use an efficient combination of pressing the dough against the board with our palms at an angle, and then squeezing the dough with our fingers as we move it back toward us.

You can knead even with arthritis in your fingers: Just lean on the dough repeatedly with your knuckles. In fact, we've been told that the working of warm dough can be beneficial to sore finger joints.

Any technique will work that presses dough against dough. What doesn't work is pulling the dough apart, so don't pull.

Comfort is important in kneading. We had a student who insisted that her arms got too tired to knead. The problem was not with her arms but with her legs: She was short and the table she kneaded on was high. She moved the dough to a lower surface, and—magic!— no more tiredness.

Make certain your kneading surface is low enough that you don't have to pull your elbows way high to knead. But, on the other hand, it should not be so low that you have to bend over; that will bother your back.

Most kneaders use a wooden board. We do, too, for the majority of breads. But for doughs that have to stay soft—that is, with as little flour as possible worked in—we use a round marble tabletop, about 20 inches in diameter. Dough doesn't stick to marble as much as it does to wood.

A thick piece of glass with beveled edges is also excellent. Any glass store will sell you a piece 24 inches square and ⅜ inch thick.

We knew a teacher who called kneaded breads her "mad" breads. Well, you don't have to be pumping adrenaline, or pumping iron, to be a successful kneader. Children can knead, old folks can knead, anyone who wishes to devote the time (and perhaps some imagination) to it can knead.

If you knead with the aid of a dough hook or a food processor, it is tempting to let the machine do all the work. But you will get a bread that is less fluffy and more satisfying if you resist the temptation. Generally, reserve some of the flour and allow the machine to work only until the dough begins to pull away from the sides of the bowl or container, then remove the dough and finish kneading by hand. We would not use a machine at all for Brioches, Challah, or Croissants. But we would allow a dough hook to do all the kneading for Italian Bread.

Preliminary Beating

To save ourselves some hand labor, we beat the thin batter of some yeast breads with an electric mixer (either hand-held or stationary). This develops some elasticity early—before the work of kneading begins. If you have no mixer (nor an eggbeater), do this early beating with a whisk or wooden spoon, but double the beating time.

How Much Is Enough Flour?

When does a dough have "enough" flour kneaded into it? That will vary from bread to bread. Italian Bread calls for more flour than French Bread does because Italian Bread requires a firmer, stiffer dough.

In general, though, a dough has enough flour in it when it stops sticking to your cleaned-off hands and can be formed into a cohesive mass: something you can hold in one hand, palm down, while it falls slowly to the board.

When there is enough flour, the dough will have a smooth feeling as you rub a hand over its surface.

When the dough has enough flour (in each recipe we give a rough idea of how much that is), continue to knead for the prescribed time (more or less; it depends on the vigor of your kneading, remember), flouring your hands or the board very lightly as you continue.

After the prescribed kneading time, the dough should have quite a smooth feel to it, and should show, when you look at the surface, the characteristic *light wrinkles* that are the mark of sufficient kneading.

Also, the dough should spring back fairly quickly when you push it down.

If you are not certain after putting in the required time, knead for another minute or two. You can hurt a dough by overkneading, but you have to overknead a *lot* before it becomes dry and unresponsive, while only a little *under*kneading will produce a sagging disaster.

The Effects of Humidity

The higher the humidity (that is, the moisture content of the air), the more flour a recipe will use. On rainy days, we often reduce the liquid in a recipe by a couple of tablespoons.

RISING

Most breads rise. Not all. For example, Tortillas, Chappatis, and Corn Dodger stay flat. But most breads in this book rise.

Yeast Breads

These breads are risen by the fermenting action of yeast. The yeasts we use in baking are actually microscopic living organisms. In the package they are dormant—asleep. When we wet them, that wakes them. When we give them something to eat, they multiply. Flour makes them multiply slowly; sugars make them multiply quickly. Salt will slow them down some—a lot of salt can kill them. High heat also kills the yeast plants (at over 140°F., they begin to die), but gentle heat stimulates them to even greater multiplication.

As they eat, they give off bubbles of carbon dioxide as a by-product (fermentation). The elasticity we've developed in the dough by kneading allows the dough to hold the bubbles, which expand like tiny balloons. The baking expands these bubbles even further.

When the baking solidifies the dough—cooks it through—the expansion stops.

If left to their own devices, the yeast plants would make carbon dioxide at a leisurely pace—or, if your kitchen is cool or the recipe calls for the bread to rise in the refrigerator, an extremely slow pace. To encourage the yeast to work faster, the dough should be put in a large bowl in a very warm place (an ambient temperature of at least 90°F.). That place could be on a trivet over the pilot light on your gas range, with a towel for a cover. A country friend uses a large rock in the summer sun.

Our favorite rising place is our sink. We stop up the sink, then run in a couple of inches of very hot water (about 140°F.). Since our mixing bowls are thick, they can sit directly in the water. (If your bowl is thin, put something into the sink to hold the bowl just over the water.) Next, we cover the sink with a couple of large cookie sheets or a thick towel.

In a covered sink, *dough rises well and quickly because the heat and the moisture really surround it*. With most other methods, heat comes only from below, and there is no moisture.

If you try the sink method, don't panic if a little water gets onto a loaf or into a pan: Just pour it off. We have seen completely drowned loaves bake up very satisfactorily.

If your sink is too small, run a few inches of hot water into your bathtub. In a tub, you don't even need a cover; just make certain doors and windows are closed against drafts.

Other alternatives? In winter, cover a radiator with a thin board or a piece of fieldstone; then a bowl of dough (or loaves in pans) can be placed on the board or stone, and covered with a towel. Dough can also be risen on the top of a television set, radio, or a stereo. The unscrambler on our cable TV set-up generates a constant gentle heat that will rise dough. It is a little slower than a sink rise, but still quite satisfactory.

DOUBLING: Most of our yeast recipes call for the dough to rise until it "doubles in volume," or "doubles in bulk." This means that the dough is expected to increase its volume by 100 percent before it is ready to be punched down.

If you are not certain what a 100 percent increase in volume looks like, do this easy exercise. Take a large mixing bowl and pour 5 cups of water into it. This is about the volume of the dough in many bread recipes. Observe where that comes to in your bowl. Now add another 5 cups of water and look again. You have just "doubled" the bulk or volume of your imaginary bowl of dough. The rising bowl should be large enough to hold this doubling—and a bit more.

THE FINGER TEST: To find out if the dough has risen enough, insert a floured finger about one joint's worth into the dough, near the edge of the bowl, not the center. If the hole does not fill, the dough is ready—that is the finger test.

PUNCHING DOWN: Many of the yeast-risen recipes call for the dough to be "punched down" after it has risen in the bowl. How do you punch down? Make a fist and punch right down into the center of the dough! The dough will make a soft hissing sound as most of the air escapes. And that is just what you want to do—get the air out.

After you have punched, knead the dough for a minute or less to get out what remains of the larger bubbles—until the dough is back to its original size. This helps to give you an even texture.

Quick Breads

Quick Breads (so-called because they mix up quickly and need no rising time—they bake no faster than yeast breads) are risen by chemical interaction.

Baking soda, a base or alkaline substance, forms bubbles when it comes into contact with an acid substance (such as yogurt) in the batter. These bubbles give some rise to the batter, and the rise is solidified when the bread is baked.

Baking powder forms similar bubbles when it is wet and then heated. The bread then rises in the same way baking soda breads do.

Neither baking soda nor baking powder gives you that marvelous yeast smell that cries out "baking!" to so many people. And they won't give you the yeast taste, or the texture of yeast breads. But they are simple to use.

It is important to remember not to use more baking soda or less yogurt in a baking soda bread than is called for in the recipes: That could leave you with a chemical taste in the bread. Too much baking powder can also leave a bad taste.

Egg Rises

Popovers rise just from eggs: no yeast, no chemicals. The egg batter holds the tiny bubbles beaten into it, and these bubbles expand with the heat.

Other breads that have eggs beaten into the batter, such as Brioches and Challah, get some of their high-rise from the eggs.

TESTING FOR DONENESS

We test for doneness of the finished bread with various tools: a thin, clean knife, a wire cake tester, a toothpick, and various parts of our anatomy—eyes, nose, hands.

KNIFE TEST: With a clean towel covering your free hand, take the bread out of the oven, turn it out of its pan into your toweled hand, and insert a clean thin knife *into the bottom of the loaf*, through almost to the top. Pull out the knife and look at the blade. Is the blade clean? Then the bread is done. Are there streaks of dough showing? Then return the loaf to its pan and the pan to the oven and continue baking.

Is it unclear whether you have moisture or dough on your knife? Wipe the knife gently on the towel. If the streaks wipe off, it was water and the bread is done. If not, the streaks are really dough, and the loaf goes back in.

CAKE TESTER: Insert this thin stiff wire into the loaf through the top, and examine in the same way as you did the knife. This is a less destructive test: the slit made by the knife test never heals. But the cake tester is often harder to read because of the thinness of the wire.

TOOTHPICK TEST: We use a toothpick on rolls, braids, and Brioches. When we think the bread is done, we take a clean, round toothpick and insert it into one of the joints of the bread: that is, where the braids overlap, or where the topknot of the Brioche joins the main body of the bread. Then we examine it for uncooked dough as with the knife or cake tester.

EYES: Get to know what a bread looks like when it approaches doneness. While you cannot tell by just looking if a loaf is done—

a bread can be brown outside and raw inside—if it looks done, that is a good time to make your first test.

NOSE: Bread smells like *bread* as it approaches doneness. This is not definitive, but, again, a strong aroma says "test."

EARS: You can tell if a loaf is done by thumping the bottom. A done loaf will usually sound somewhat hollow; a loaf with raw dough inside will usually make a flat thud when you thump its bottom. Granted, this takes a little practice.

HIGH-ALTITUDE BAKING

For you yeast bakers whose ovens are at 3,000 feet or higher, Faye Egan, manager of the Nabisco Brands Kitchens, gave us the results of their experiments at high altitudes. To avoid overrising, reduce your yeast by a half teaspoon for every package or tablespoon of yeast in the recipe. No temperature change is required.

NOTES

Let's face it, your baking experiences will vary from ours. However seldom and in however small a degree, there will be differences. Make pencil notes right in this book, right on the recipes themselves, or you will be surprised every time. This is one of the advantages of owning a book. If your experiences are substantially different from our instructions, let us know.

TIMING

Recipes get timed from the moment you put the bread in the oven. A bread starting in a cold oven is timed from the put-in, not from when the oven hits full temperature.

Ovens vary. Do make notes on how long individual breads take until they test done *in your oven*. If you get a new oven, start a whole new set of notes.

COOLING

Breads coming hot from the oven will condense moisture under the loaf and soften the bottom crust. We put the bread on a wire rack so that air can circulate and the water can evaporate.

TEMPERATURE OF INGREDIENTS

There is no aspect of baking where you will find more difference of opinion among recipe writers than in the area of temperatures. We will not try to resolve these differences, but will tell you what *we* mean when we give you a temperature for a liquid or for rising dough.

Liquid temperatures are easily measured with a candy thermometer. We use a finger, and after a little baking, you will too.

"*Hot*" liquid is between 125° and 140°F.

"*Warm*" liquid is about 100° to 110°F.

"*Very warm*" liquid fills the niche between those two.

A "*very warm*" *place for rising dough* should provide a surrounding temperature of over 100°F. (Since it is easier to keep a liquid hot than the air around it, a covered sink with a few inches of hot tap water provides a good deal of ambient warmth for rising a bowl of dough.)

By "*room temperature*" we mean 70° to 75°F.

Except where otherwise indicated, ingredients should be at room temperature or warmer before they are added to yeast. Even baking-powder- or baking-soda-risen recipes will take longer to bake if the ingredients are combined cold.

MEASUREMENTS

Bread baking is not an exact science. Except for Popovers and Croissants, if you never used a measuring spoon or cup, so long as you used the *same* tablespoon and teacup all the time, you would probably have success every time you baked one of our recipes. But many people need the support of science, and so we recommend the following measuring devices.

A nest of measuring spoons comes in very handy, especially when measuring small amounts of things like salt.

We use both a 1-cup and a 2-cup glass measure. A 2-cup measure is desirable when you are measuring more than 1 cup of liquid in total. Often, all the liquid ingredients can be measured together into the same cup before they are added to the dry ingredients. This is a more accurate way of measuring because, except for water, we can seldom pour all the liquid out of the measure.

Here's a hint: If you are measuring oil and honey into the same recipe, measure the oil into the cup first, then add the honey to the oil in the measure. Then scrape it all out. This way, the oil keeps the honey from sticking to the sides of the measure.

ORDER OF INGREDIENTS

There is nothing sacred about the order in which we present the ingredients in a recipe. Experience has shown us that our order works. But, if you prefer, change the order.

Of course, if you decide, for example, to put the yeast in last you will have some interesting experiences. However, you *can* get bread that way.

PAN SIZE

Wherever possible, use a pan of the size and shape called for: The recipes have been standardized for those sizes and shapes.

However, if you must substitute, keep these rules of thumb in mind.

Do not substitute a larger pan—that way lies failure. The breads will not rise as high in a larger pan, and they will take longer to bake. The first means that the breads will be heavier; the second means that the breads will be drier.

By all means, substitute smaller pans if you must. Usually, three smaller pans can be substituted for two larger pans, but do not fill the smaller pans as full as instructed for larger pans: In smaller pans, dough rises more. Reduce the baking time in small pans by about five minutes. If you have too much dough for the pans, make rolls of the excess (or muffins, if the recipe is for a quick bread).

Any recipe for a bread in a shaped pan can be baked in a loaf pan. But many shaped pans have a central post, which speeds up baking. And, since shaped pans have more surface, they usually take a smaller thickness of dough. If you wish to abandon the shaped pan, think small. You may substitute two small loaf pans for one shaped pan.

WHISK AND BEATER CLEANING

It is difficult to clean a whisk that has been used for beating batter by just scraping. The best way to reclaim that batter from the whisk is to put some flour into a separate container, dip the whisk into it, and rub the whisk clean with your hand, allowing the rubbings to fall into the bowl. If you need to, dip and rub a second time. The same technique works with electric beaters, wooden spoons— and your fingers! Or you can pour some flour into your palm and rub it over the bowl.

FLOURS

Flour is the finely ground berries (seeds) of various grasses and legumes. Every flour made from whole grains must be stored in a refrigerator or the oil it contains will become rancid.

Wheat

Wheat flour is the basic bread flour because it contains *gluten*. Gluten is a protein substance which can be worked up to an elastic state that holds the bubbles created by the yeast, allowing the bread to rise.

The wheat berry, like all the grass grains, is made up of three parts: the coarse outer layer, called the *bran*; the embryo or *germ* (the "live" part that, given a chance, would sprout into a new plant); and the starchy inner part, which would be the food supply of the seed, the endosperm.

When millers remove the bran and wheat germ (see below) to make white flour, they remove 90 percent of the fiber—mostly in the bran—and about twenty-five vitamins and minerals. Sometimes they "enrich" the flour before marketing it, but they return only four vitamins—and three of those in smaller amounts than what was removed. They do add iron, however, which is not found in the whole, unrefined wheat.

After the removal of the bran and germ often comes bleaching, a process wherein a gas is forced through the flour to whiten it further.

White flour has nutritional deficiencies, but there is no question that white flour gives you a finer-textured bread than whole wheat flour does.

White flour is lighter, fluffier, less absorbent, easier to shape, and quicker to rise. There are some breads you just can't make with whole wheat flour. As an experiment, we tried to make Brioches with whole wheat. The flavor was fine, but the texture? It just wasn't Brioches. The same is true of Challah. Even Popovers don't pop as high.

What to do? Our solution is to bake whole wheat breads as our everyday breads, and to substitute wheat germ and/or bran for some of the white flour in every white bread we bake.

Wheat flour comes in several forms:

WHOLE WHEAT FLOUR, OR GRAHAM FLOUR: This flour contains all the bran and all the germ from the wheat berry, and so must be stored in the refrigerator. It is rich in B and E vitamins and contains many other nutrients (not iron, though).

The preferable form of whole wheat flour is stone-ground (see glossary).

Two caveats: (1) If your flour is labeled "organic," be certain your source is a reliable one. (2) Be certain the whole wheat flour you buy is not *brominated*—treated with bromine gas as a preservative, a process which kills the wheat germ and hence destroys some of the flour's nutritive value. Brominating is done to increase the shelf-life of unrefrigerated whole wheat.

UNBLEACHED ENRICHED WHITE FLOUR: This flour gives you the textural advantages of white flour without the chemical residues left behind by bleaching and brominating. A few nutrients have been returned as described above. This is the only "white" flour we use; it has a creamy off-white color.

WHEAT GERM FLOUR: Unbleached enriched white flour that has had some wheat germ returned to it. This is a better flour than unbleached white, but we prefer to add our own wheat germ.

BLEACHED ENRICHED WHITE FLOUR (also called *All-Purpose Flour*): The bleaching is done to make the flour whiter. The flour may be brominated as well. We don't use bleached flour at all.

UNENRICHED BLEACHED FLOUR: This flour, used in many commercial bread and pizza bakeries, has all the nutritional value of library paste.

PASTRY FLOUR: Made from a variety of low-gluten wheat, pastry flour is inappropriate for kneaded breads but is okay in quick breads.

GLUTEN FLOUR: Gluten flour is about 50 percent protein. It is usually reserved for people on special diets. Gluten flour produces a bread with a poor texture.

BRAN: The bran is the part richest in fiber. It also contains B vitamins, and nearly 20 percent of the protein in the wheat seed.

WHEAT GERM: The wheat germ contains polyunsaturated oil, B vitamins, vitamin E, and about 10 percent of the protein in the wheat seed. Wheat germ is available raw or toasted. Since it is cooked in the baking in any case, we use whichever form is more convenient. Wheat germ must be stored in the refrigerator.

CRACKED WHEAT: Cracked wheat is the wheat berry cracked into large chunks, and you might as well try to knead bird gravel. Commercial "cracked wheat bread" is white bread with a little cracked wheat added.

WHEAT GRITS: This is like cracked wheat, but broken into smaller bits. While both are unsuitable as a major ingredient in a bread, both make nice textural additions.

Other Grains

BARLEY: This grain is more commonly used in making alcoholic beverages than in bread, but it is sweet and the flour is especially useful as a substitute for part of the wheat flour in quick breads.

BUCKWHEAT: This is one of the few grains we use that is not a grass. Buckwheat has less protein than wheat, but about as much as corn does. The flour has a strong flavor, a grayish look, and a fine texture. It can be used alone in pancakes and quick breads, but it contains too little gluten to be useful except as an additive in yeast breads.

CORN: In this book we use both corn flour and cornmeal. *Cornmeal* is available in several different coarsenesses—unmarked. The best texture comes with stone grinding of yellow corn. White cornmeal is finer, and not terribly helpful in recipes calling for real crunch. We used to be able to get *stone-ground* yellow cornmeal from an historic mill—and it was the best we ever used.

The *corn flour* we use in Tortillas is Masa Harina (from the

Quaker Company). This is steel ground, but has no preservatives added. Before grinding, the corn kernels are soaked in water in which limestone has been dissolved, which softens the seed jacket and makes for a distinctive flavor.

OATS: Horses eat more oats than people do. But *oatmeal, rolled oats*, and *oat flour* make very nice sweet additions to breads, substituted for less than a quarter of the wheat flour. Oats gives a sweet flavor to a bread, and it has a natural preservative which helps bread to keep longer.

RICE: *Rice flour* is hard to find, but it has a lovely texture and an interesting flavor. Of course, you want brown-rice flour, which is a whole-grain flour.
Rice polish is the outer covering of the rice grain: what has been ground off to turn healthful brown rice into white rice. Rice polish is rich in B vitamins.

RYE: After wheat, this is the most popular of the bread grains—though in this country it is more often grown as a cover crop than as a food grain. The flour is low in gluten, but a lot of kneading will develop the gluten that it has. Rye has a sharpish, piquant taste that is inappropriate in sweet breads but great in sandwich breads.

SOY: This is actually a legume, not a grass. The flour contains B vitamins and a lot of protein, but no gluten. Substitute only a little of it in yeast breads, but as much as your taste dictates in quick breads.

SUBSTITUTIONS: For added nutrition, flavor, or textural interest, you can substitute as much as a half cup of bran, wheat germ, cracked wheat, wheat grits, barley flour, buckwheat flour, cornmeal, oat flour, rice flour, rice polish, or rye flour in any yeast-bread recipe.

YEASTS

Yeasts—which are living microorganisms, remember—have been used by humans since the dawn of history—and earlier. The alcohol in all fermented drinks is created as a by-product of yeast life processes.

The Bible records that Noah got drunk—presumably on something fermented. And in the desert, the children of Israel had to make do with *un*leavened bread—so, clearly, they usually ate leavened (yeast-risen) bread.

Skipping down the ages to relatively modern times, brewers have kept strains of yeast alive for generations. Great-grandma baked with live brewer's yeast* which she got from her local brewer.

By the late nineteenth century, Grandma was able to buy prepackaged yeast, a live strain related to but not identical to, brewer's yeast, with the yeast living in a dryish medium that was mostly starch. By keeping this "cake yeast" cool and dry, she was able to keep a supply of it in her kitchen—until it went moldy.

One of the technological wonders to come out of World War II was active dry yeast, which lasts for many months in a dormant state (so long as it is kept dry: Wetting it brings it to life). When we first wrote *Bake Your Own Bread*, Fleischmann's used a preservative in their packages of active dry yeast. We complained to them and to the world. They no longer use preservatives.

The newest developments in yeast are the quick-rising yeasts, which cut down the rising time of breads by about 50 percent without altering flavor or texture.

SUBSTITUTING QUICK-RISING YEASTS FOR ACTIVE DRY: To substitute Fleischmann's RapidRise for active dry yeast, combine the yeast with some of the flour, stir, and mix in hot liquid (about 125° F.), then add the remaining ingredients as you normally would. The yeast has begun to work.

Red Star's Quick-Rise can be substituted in the same way, or you can simply replace the active dry yeast in a recipe with the Quick-Rise, and proceed according to the original recipe directions, mixing the yeast with water.

With either brand, the rising time will be cut by about half.

---

* Don't confuse this with the nutritional supplement also called brewer's yeast—or the related strain, torula yeast. This strong-flavored stuff has no effect on the rising of bread because the yeast plants are *dead*. As an additive to a recipe, however, it can make a contribution to your family's health because it is very high in B vitamins and protein.

SWEETENERS

Aside from date sugar, all of the sweeteners we use are true sugars by definition. But some are better for you—and better tasting—than others.

BROWN SUGAR: White sugar to which some molasses has been added. *Light Brown Sugar* has less molasses, *dark brown sugar* has more.

DATE SUGAR: Ground-up dried dates. This is only moderately sweet, but it is a tasty and nutritious addition to dessert breads.

HONEY: The nectar gathered by bees from flowers, predigested, and then evaporated by the bees to the thick consistency with which you are familiar. Different flowers give different flavors. It is the predigestion that gives honey some unique properties. For example, honey can be digested by some people whose stomachs are too damaged to digest anything else.

Honeys have flavors that far surpass sugar, and contain, in addition, small amounts of a wide range of vitamins and minerals. Honey also has a natural preservative power that can keep your breads fresher quite a long while.

There are many therapeutic claims made for honey: we know several beekeepers who insist that honey keeps them well and young; other beekeepers have described its curative powers to us quite convincingly, and we have successfully used it as an antiseptic on several occasions.

MAPLE SUGAR: Crystalized maple syrup with much of the same great flavor. If you have old recipes calling for white sugar, substitute an equal amount of maple sugar, and enjoy the improvement.

MAPLE SYRUP: The evaporated sap of the sugar maple tree. It is rich in minerals but quite expensive. We never use the cheaper but chemicalized "maple flavored" substitutes. Maple syrup can be substituted for an equal amount of honey. The results will be less sweet but more flavorful.

MOLASSES: When cane sugar is harvested, the cane is squeezed, and the squeezings are thrown into the pot for boiling down; the heaviest particles, the ones that contain the minerals, sink to the bottom. The top layer, which is, aside from calories, nutrition-free, is refined further, crystallized, and granulated into *white sugar*.

From the middle layers is taken *light molasses* and *dark molasses*. The dark is richer in minerals than the light.

From the icky bottom layer, which contains iron and other minerals, and whatever vitamins are not heat-sensitive, is taken *blackstrap molasses*. Blackstrap will not improve the keeping power of your breads, as honey does, but it will improve its nutritional value. It has a strong, licoricey taste which does not suit everyone—but that flavor is much reduced in baking.

RAW SUGAR: The name is a misnomer. The only time you eat raw sugar is when you chew on a sugarcane. So-called raw sugar is white sugar to which about 2 percent of the removed minerals have been returned. We don't buy it because we don't find it worthwhile.

WHITE SUGAR OR GRANULATED SUGAR: Empty calories. We never use it. You cannot substitute granulated sugar for the liquid sugars (honey, molasses, maple syrup) called for in our recipes.

FATS

So far as the chemistry of bread baking is concerned, all fats that are mixed in with the other ingredients in a recipe are interchangeable: oil or butter or margarine or lard—for bread baking, other than flavor, it makes no difference. For your health, however, it makes a lot of difference.

The body cannot function properly without fats and oils. The fatty acids your body manufactures from the fats and oils you eat are vital to your life processes. However, not all fats and oils can be used by your body in this way.

Think of fats as little charms. The body links these charms together into a charm bracelet called a fatty acid. If the links of the charm are open, they are easily linked up into these fatty acid chains. If the links are already filled (with hydrogen or oxygen), they cannot readily form into fatty acid chains. Those fats with open links are "unsaturated" and desirable; those with closed links are "saturated" and undesirable.

There are several recipes in this book made without any *added* oil at all (whole grains naturally contain some unsaturated oils).

When recipes call for oil, we recommend only unsaturated (or polyunsaturated) oils: corn, soy, safflower, sesame. When buying unsaturated oils, read the labels to avoid chemical additives.

Greasing

As far as the chemistry of greasing is concerned, however, there is a great difference among fats. *Oils*, though they are generally better for you, are simply not greasy enough to keep pans from sticking. Oils soak into the dough, rather than forming a "nonstick" layer between the dough and the pan.

We generally use butter to grease our baking pans.

We formerly used margarine for greasing. Margarine was so much cheaper than butter. But we have come to the conclusion that the lower price is no bargain.

Butter is made from cream, a highly saturated fat into which air has been forced to make it solid. Sometimes salt is added (originally no doubt as a preservative, but now because so many consumers are used to the flavor).

Margarine is a combination of vegetable oils and other ingredients—often several chemicals. The oil used is often not specified. Corn and soya oils are widely used and these unsaturated oils (if not tampered with) are good food. If, however, cottonseed oil is used, insecticide residues may persist, because cotton, not considered a food, is heavily sprayed. Coconut oil, a highly saturated oil, is also sometimes used. This combination of oil and chemicals (and such other stuff as milk powder, salt, and water) is then hydrogenated to make it as saturated as butter—and then dyed to make it look like butter.

There are also "soft margarines," which contain more oil—but often more chemicals as well.

For greasing, we have opted for the less chemicaled, though no-less-saturated, choice—butter, which we usually spread on in a thin layer with our fingertips.

If you wish to avoid both butter and margarine, there is a third choice which is superior to both nutritionally, and excellent for greasing—*liquid lecithin*, a natural emulsifier. (We do not use lecithin with breads that have delicate flavors, such as popovers and croissants.)

Liquid lecithin, generally available in health food stores, is extracted from soy beans. It is unsaturated and very greasy. It looks as if it should go in your car, not on your bread pans, but do not be put off. A few drops, dripped into a pan and then spread *very* thinly and thoroughly with your fingers over every surface of the pan that touches the dough, will grease better than butter, and add no calories. There is a mild scent which usually disappears in the baking.

Pam, a spray-on product combining lecithin and corn oil, has worked fine for many of our students. We prefer to stick (or nonstick) to the pure lecithin.

MILK

Calcium absorption takes place only in the presence of some fat; therefore, children—barring allergies—should have whole milk, with some butterfat in it.

Adults, conversely, are better off having nonfat milk.

But we adults still need our calcium, and calcium deficiencies are common in the United States (we're glad the medical establishment is finally giving that some publicity). We take supplements and eat foods (such as cabbage, cauliflower, and broccoli) that are rich in calcium.

For baking, we use instant nonfat milk powder. It is convenient, keeps well, and measures easily.

In recipes calling for nonfat milk, you can use bottled nonfat milk, or mix milk powder with water beforehand. If you are baking for kids, substitute whole milk routinely. This will not affect the baking. If you use certified raw milk, then you must scald it first: raw milk contains enzymes which can inhibit yeast action.

EGGS

Eggs are a good food with a bad rap, because they contain cholesterol. They are fine protein and an excellent source of *lecithin*, which helps the body to deal with cholesterol.

In our recipes, when we call for eggs, we mean *large* eggs. If small eggs happen to be a great buy, substitute small eggs at the rate of three for two.

Eggs should always be at room temperature when they go into a bread recipe. If yours are cold from the refrigerator, submerge them in hot tap water for a few minutes.

SALT

The original edition of *Bake Your Own Bread* used only sea salt, to avoid the chemicals added to commercial salt to make it pour more easily. We still use sea salt, but less of it.

We found that when we first reduced the amount of salt in our foods, we missed it. And then our palates adjusted, and we didn't miss it. Now we find we can taste a wider range of flavors.

SOME DON'TS

Here are a few bits of "conventional wisdom" that we would like to put to rest.

BREAKING EGGS: A lot of old recipes call for you to break your eggs into a separate bowl—that was to avoid mixing the other ingredients with a bad egg. Not necessary. Of course, check to make certain the eggs are not overaged (look for the expiration date on the carton) or cracked in the box. But, really, when was the last time you got a bad egg?

PREHEATING: Do not preheat your oven unless the recipe specifies it. Many of the recipes that we have worked out start in a *cold* oven. This allows some rise to occur in the oven just before the yeast is killed.

SCALDING MILK: Milk is scalded—brought just to the simmer— to destroy enzymes that might interfere with yeast action. But, unless you use raw milk, scalding is unnecessary. Pasteurization (which also heats the milk) has already gotten rid of the enzymes.

SIFTING: We don't sift. We *pour* the flour from its bag into a measuring cup. Yes, how tightly that flour gets packed varies—but so does the amount of flour used in a bread.

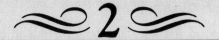
Whole Wheat Breads

WE consider whole wheat breads our everyday breads, and so, we hope, will you.

Breads made with white flour need extra ingredients added to make them nutritious. Whole wheat breads need no nutritional help—so long as you use whole wheat flour which is untreated (not brominated) and which is stone ground. These two conditions met, your whole wheat flour will contain a broad range of vitamins and minerals and proteins from the germ and the bran.

Whole wheat flour does not make a bread that rises picture-book high, nor does it give you a superfine texture.

What whole wheat flour does give you is a naturally delicious and chewy loaf of bread that looks and tastes like your image of the good life. (For a discussion of flours, see Chapter 1, page 12.)

HANDLING WHOLE WHEAT FLOUR

Whole wheat dough feels quite odd while it is being kneaded. The outside can feel dry, sticking to neither the board nor your hands, while beneath the surface it can be moist enough to make you want to force in another cupful of flour. Well, don't! Whole wheat dough just feels like that. If you force in enough flour to make the insides dry, the bread will wind up horribly heavy. The best way to handle the kneading of whole wheat dough is to dust your hands and the kneading board frequently, rather than add tablespoons of flour at a time.

Raw whole wheat dough tends to form a crust easily when rising, and so it should be kept covered with a clean, warm, *wet* towel while rising in the bowl. (Soak a dishtowel in hot water and wring it out.) This will keep a damp atmosphere around the rising dough and prevent the surface from drying out.

Tan breads, that is, breads made with both whole wheat and white flours, rise higher than whole wheat but not as high as white breads.

◇ *If you've never kneaded before, read Kneading (page 1), before you begin.*

◇ *Whole wheat flour is more absorbent than white flour; if you try to adapt a white flour recipe to whole wheat, you'll wind up using less flour.*

Rich Whole Wheat Bread

It's easy enough to see why we call this good-keeper of a bread "Rich Whole Wheat." It has lots of eggs, milk, and oil—and the calories that go with them. But what a delicious and healthful way to get them.

◇ *If you want to use whole milk instead of the hot water and milk powder, warm the milk to about 125°F.*

◇ *Make "Superbread" by substituting ½ cup of wheat germ and ½ cup of bran for 1 cup of flour, at about cup 4.*

◇ *For additional vitamins and minerals, substitute blackstrap molasses for all or part of the honey.*

◇ *Add the grated zest of 1 lemon to "brighten" the flavor.*

◇ *Knead in 1 cup of unsulfured raisins when you shape the loaves, or ½ to 1 cup of any dried fruit, nut, or seed combination that strikes your fancy. Sunflower seeds combined with raisins are great in this bread.*

◇ *See also the suggestions for flour and grain substitutions on page 15.*

◇ *This bread also makes excellent rolls—see recipe page 86.*

MAKES 3 LOAVES IN 8½-INCH PANS

2 packages active dry yeast
1 tablespoon salt
¼ cup unsaturated oil
¼ cup honey
2½ cups hot water (125°F., see page 9)

1 cup nonfat milk powder
2 cups whole wheat flour
3 large eggs at room temperature
6 to 7 cups whole wheat flour (additional)

Into a large mixing bowl, measure the yeast, salt, oil, honey, and hot water. Stir.

Mix in the milk powder.

Add the 2 cups of flour and mix with a wooden spoon until the batter is fairly smooth.

One at a time, beat in the eggs well.

Beat in 5 cups of the additional flour, 1 cup at a time. Beat in each cup well before adding the next.

Spread cup 8 onto your kneading board, scrape the dough out onto it, turn the dough over, and knead the flour in. Continue to knead in small amounts of additional flour until the dough stops sticking.

Knead for another 10 to 15 minutes.

When the dough is kneaded, pour a tablespoon of oil into the scraped-out mixing bowl, add the dough, then turn it to oil all sides.

Cover with a warm, wet towel, and set to rise in a warm, draft-free place for 1 to 1½ hours until the dough has at least doubled in bulk and passes the finger test (see page 6).

When risen, punch the dough down, then knead for a minute in the bowl to get rid of the larger bubbles.

Divide the dough into three pieces and shape each piece into a loaf.

Grease well three 8½-inch loaf pans and put one loaf in each pan.

Cover each loaf with a warm, wet towel, and put to rise in a warm, draft-free place for about half the time of the first rise.

When the loaves are well risen, put into a cold oven set for 375°F., and bake for about 40 minutes, or until the loaves test done (see page 7).

Turn the loaves out of the pans, and cool on a wire rack.

100% Whole Wheat Bread

This is a water bread—no eggs or oil—and like any water bread it will dry out in a few days. However, because of the preservative power of the honey, it never tastes stale and it resists mold. It is a marvelous sandwich bread.

◊ *For added iron, substitute blackstrap molasses for the honey. This gives you a darker bread with more vitamins and minerals—but the molasses has no preservative power.*

◊ *For an extra little zing, add the grated zest of half an orange or lemon, kneading it in well when you shape the loaves.*

◊ *One cup of unsulfured raisins can be kneaded in before shaping the loaves.*

◊ *For extra calcium, add 1 cup of nonfat milk powder, but if you do, don't change the amount of water.*

◊ *If you wish to juggle flours, using ½ cup of this and ¼ cup of that, go right ahead. The only limit is your imagination—and the knowledge that you don't want to make more than 1 cup of substitutions.*

◊ *We recommend such coarse grain substitutes as ½ cup of cracked wheat, wheat grits, rye meal, or cornmeal. Buckwheat flour has a strong flavor, but it blends in well in small amounts.*

MAKES 3 LOAVES IN 8-INCH PANS

2 packages active dry yeast
¼ cup honey
2 teaspoons salt

3 cups hot water (about 125°F., see page 9)
6½ to 7½ cups whole wheat flour

Into a large bowl, measure the yeast, honey, salt, and water, and stir well.

Add 4 cups of the flour, 1 cup at a time, stirring each cup in well.

Add a fifth cup of flour to the bowl and beat thoroughly with a wooden spoon.

Spread the sixth cup of flour over the kneading board, scrape the dough onto the flour, turn the dough over, and work the flour in.

Sprinkle another ½ cup of flour over the dough; knead it in.

Knead in as much of another cup of flour as required to make the dough stop sticking to the board.

Now, knead easily for another 15 minutes, or vigorously for 10 minutes, dusting your hands or the board lightly with flour as the dough sticks.

When those characteristic light wrinkles appear on the surface of the dough (see page 3), it's ready.

Pour a teaspoon of oil into the scraped-out mixing bowl, drop in the dough, and turn it to oil all surfaces.

Cover with a clean, warm, wet towel, and put in a warm, draft-free place to rise for an hour or more, until the dough has at least doubled in volume and passes the finger test (see page 6).

When the dough is ready, punch it down and then knead it gently in the bowl for a minute to get rid of the larger bubbles.

Divide the dough into three equal parts and shape each piece into a loaf.

If you want smooth end slices, chop straight down close to the end of the loaf with the edge of your hand. This "karate chop" (see below) will leave a small flap of dough, which should be tucked under the end of the loaf. Repeat at the other end.

Grease well three 8-inch loaf pans, and place one loaf in each pan. Or you can make freestanding loaves and put them on two greased baking sheets.

Once the loaves are in the pans, cover each with a damp towel and put into that warm, draft-free place to rise for half the time of the first rise, until the dough is risen above the rims of the pans.

Starting in a cold oven set for 375°F., bake for 40 minutes, until the bread tests done (see page 7).

If the bread tests undone but the crust shows signs of scorching, shut the oven off and allow the bread to sit in the oven for another 5 to 10 minutes.

Turn the loaves out of the pans, and cool briefly on a wire rack, but by all means serve some hot if possible.

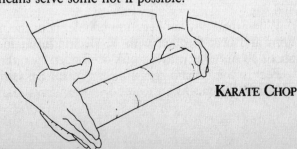

KARATE CHOP

Dark Whole Wheat Cinnamon-Raisin Bread

Whole wheat breads tend to be heavy, and raisins just weigh them down more—so we have substituted 2 cups of white flour for 2 cups of the whole wheat in this recipe. This makes for a bread that is easier to knead and one that rises better.

◊ *To help the rising along, we allow the yeast to get a "running start" by combining it with the water and molasses and allowing it to stand. (When it froths, don't be afraid.)*
◊ *You can cut down on rising time by about a third by substituting a quick-rising yeast (see page 16).*

MAKES 3 LOAVES IN 7-INCH PANS

1½ cups unsulfured raisins
1 cup hot water (about 125°F., see page 9)
½ cup dark molasses
2 packages active dry yeast
2 cups unbleached enriched white flour

½ teaspoon salt
2 tablespoons powdered cinnamon
¼ cup unsaturated oil
2 large eggs, at room temperature
5 cups whole wheat flour

Soak the raisins in a cup of hot tap water for about 15 minutes.

Drain the raisin water into a measuring cup. (Save the raisins for later.) Add enough hot water to bring the raisin water to 1 cup.

Combine the raisin water with the molasses, then add the yeast and stir all together. Allow to stand until bubbling action begins—as little as 5 minutes.

Measure the white flour, salt, and cinnamon into a large bowl and stir.

When the yeast has begun to bubble, pour the mixture over the flour and beat together with an electric mixer for 5 minutes (or about 10 minutes with a whisk or wooden spoon).

Beat in the oil and eggs until the mixture is fairly uniform.

Mix in the raisins.

Add 1 cup of the whole wheat flour and beat for 2 minutes (4 minutes by hand).

Switch over to a wooden spoon and stir in, ½ cup at a time, 3 more cups of whole wheat flour.

Sprinkle about ¼ cup whole wheat flour on the kneading board, and scrape the dough onto it. Sprinkle another ¼ cup of flour over the dough and work it in gently.

Knead for a total of about 8 to 10 minutes, flouring lightly as you knead. Work in as much of the last cup of flour as required to make the dough easy to handle and quite elastic—*but not dry*. The dough should spring back when you push it, but it should change its shape readily if you pick it up.

Pour a tablespoon of oil into the scraped-out mixing bowl, put the dough in, and turn it over to oil all sides.

Cover with a warm, wet towel, and put to rise in a warm, draft-free place until at least doubled in bulk—about 1½ hours.

When risen, knead the dough gently in the bowl to get rid of the larger bubbles. Divide the dough into three equal parts, and form each piece into a loaf shape.

Grease well three 7-inch loaf pans, and place one loaf into each pan.

Cover loaves with a warm, wet towel and put to rise again until the dough fills the pans—about 40 minutes.

Starting in a cold oven set at 375°F., bake for about 35 minutes, or until the loaves are browned on top and test done (see page 7).

Turn the loaves out of the pans, and cool on a wire rack.

Sprouted Wheat Bread

"Sprouted" is a misnomer; the wheat berries (wheat seeds) are soaked for two days in advance, which softens them enough not to chip your teeth, and leaves them chewy, but does not quite sprout them.

◊ *Wheat berries can be bought at a health food store.*

MAKES 2 LOAVES IN 7-INCH PANS

½ cup wheat berries
2 packages active dry yeast
1½ cups warm water (about 110°F., see page 9)

¼ cup dark molasses
1 teaspoon salt
4¼ cups whole wheat flour

Soak the wheat berries in 2 cups of water for two days. (Change the water after the first day.) This will yield 1 cup of softened berries.

When the grains of wheat are softened, combine the yeast with the warm water and molasses. Stir, and then allow to stand for a few minutes, until yeast bubbles begin to form.

Measure the salt and 2 cups of the flour into a large bowl, and stir in the yeast mixture.

Beat for 7 minutes with an electric beater (about 15 minutes with a wooden spoon) to develop the elasticity.

Switch over to a wooden spoon, and, ½ cup at a time, beat in an additional 1½ cups of flour.

Sprinkle about ¼ cup of flour on your kneading board, scrape the dough out onto it, and sprinkle another ¼ cup over the top. Begin to work in this flour.

Knead for a total of 8 to 10 minutes, using as much as required of the final ¼ cup of flour to make a light and elastic dough.

Put a teaspoon of oil into the scraped-out mixing bowl, put in the dough, and turn it to oil all sides.

Cover with a warm, wet towel and set to rise in a warm, draft-free place, until doubled in volume—about 1 hour, or until it passes the finger test (page 6).

Drain the wheat berries and pat them dry on a paper towel.

Grease well two 7-inch baking pans.

When risen, punch the dough down in the bowl. Spread the dough over the bottom of the bowl, sprinkle in the berries, and knead for a minute or so in the bowl, until the grains are well worked in. Dust your hands lightly with flour, if necessary, to keep from sticking.

Divide the dough in half, shape into rough loaves, and put each half into a pan.

Cover each loaf with a warm, wet towel and set to rise again for about ½ hour, until the loaves just about fill the pans.

Preheat your oven to 375°F., and bake for about 35 minutes, or until the loaves test done (see page 7). Do not overbake.

Turn the loaves out of the pans, and cool on a wire rack.

Whole Wheat Italian Bread Sticks (Grissini)

These bread sticks are like a visit to a good Italian restaurant, one that does its own baking—with whole wheat flour.

This recipe also makes a wonderful pizza dough (see page 99).

◊ *For a snappier taste, add 1 teaspoon of fresh-ground black pepper.*
◊ *For a plainer stick, omit the herbs.*
◊ *Sesame seeds are the traditional finish, but poppy seeds work fine, too, as does garlic powder.*

MAKES ABOUT 60 9-INCH STICKS

The Dough:

1 package active dry yeast
¾ cup hot water (about 125°F., see page 9)
1½ cups whole wheat flour
1 teaspoon salt
1 large egg, at room temperature

¼ cup olive oil
1 teaspoon dried crushed rosemary
1 teaspoon dried chopped sage
2 cups whole wheat flour (additional)

The Glaze:

1 large egg
1 tablespoon water

¼ cup sesame seeds

Dissolve the yeast in the water, and allow to stand for a few minutes.

Measure the 1½ cups of flour and the salt into a large bowl, add the dissolved yeast and water, and stir until wet.

Beat with an electric mixer for about 3 minutes (or with a whisk or wooden spoon for about 6 minutes).

Beat in the egg for a minute, then the oil for a minute, then the herbs.

Stir in 1¼ cups of the additional flour with a wooden spoon, ¼ cup at a time, until all the flour is wet.

Sprinkle a couple of tablespoons of flour on the kneading board, scrape the dough over it, and sprinkle another 2 tablespoons of flour on top. Begin to knead gently.

Knead in as much of the final ½ cup of flour as required to make the dough medium-stiff but quite smooth, about 5 to 7 minutes. (This brings the flour to a total of 3½ cups.)

Pour a tablespoon of olive oil into the scraped-out mixing bowl, put in the dough, and turn it to oil all sides.

Cover with a warm, wet towel and set to rise in a warm, draft-free place, for about 1 hour—or until it is doubled in volume and passes the finger test (page 6).

When risen, punch the dough down, and knead briefly and gently in the bowl.

Grease two large baking sheets.

Divide the dough in half, sprinkle a little flour on the kneading board, and roll out one of the halves to a 10-inch square, about ⅛ inch thick.

Cut the square into strips about ½ inch wide, and cut the strips in half. (This gives you 5-inch strips that are ½ inch wide.) Now, roll them out to about pinky thickness (about ⅜ inch) and approximately 9 inches long.

Place the strips on the baking sheets, with about an inch between each.

Set the strips to rise, covered with warm, wet towels, at room temperature (70°F. minimum) for about 30 minutes, or until they are visibly risen (they do not rise a lot).

Preheat your oven to 400°F.

Prepare the glaze: Beat the egg and water together with a fork until smooth. When the sticks are risen, remove the towels and brush on the egg, covering all visible dough. Sprinkle with sesame seeds.

Bake for 25 to 27 minutes, or until the sticks are crisp but not scorched.

Place on a wire rack until cool.

White Breads

WHITE breads are the texture champs. They knead up easily (and with less sticking than whole wheat breads) and rise high, wide, and handsome.

But white flour, though it has been enriched, is nutritionally second-class food because it lacks the fiber of the bran and the vitamin E of the germ. We suggest that you routinely substitute about a half cup of wheat germ or bran (or a quarter cup of each) in all your white bread recipes.

◊ *If you've never kneaded before, read Kneading (page 1), before you begin.*

French Bread

This is really a "convertible" bread (a hardtop convertible—it has a great crust!). It has multi-ethnic origins. The way we treat it in this recipe, it is undoubtedly French. But we can buy the same bread with a paler top in Spanish Harlem in New York, and there it is called Cuban Bread. On Nantucket, the loaf is almost white and rounder, and it is Portuguese Bread.

The loaf you make for yourself here is about as close to the bread you might buy from a commercial baker as a live bird is to a stuffed bird. You have to go to France to get French bread this good, and it's getting tougher to find there, too.

◊ *To develop a good crust, we spray the loaves with water three times (we use a clean mister) and leave a pan of water in the bottom of the oven during baking to raise the humidity.*

◊ *The cornmeal on the baking sheets gives the loaves a crunchy bottom—the only place we can't reach with the spray.*

◊ *Don't be misled by the small size of the unbaked dough loaves before they rise—they will rise plenty.*

◊ *If you routinely add salt at the table, you may want to increase the salt in the recipe to 1 tablespoon, or spray with salty water.*

◊ *Vegetable cooking water can be substituted for the hot water in the recipe—as can chicken soup.*

◊ *Whole wheat flour can be substituted for up to two thirds of the white flour—but you won't get quite as much rise.*

◊ *Or as much as 1 cup of wheat germ or bran can be substituted for an equal amount of flour.*

◊ *If you wish to bake only two baguettes, store half the dough in a covered bowl in the refrigerator (see page 232). When you want the dough, knead it down and allow it to come to room temperature before shaping. The extra rise is all to the good.*

◊ *These French baguettes require diagonal slashing. If you are making round loaves, slash in the form of a tic-tac-toe—two slashes across and two down. For Viennese Bread, make 1 long slash down the center.*

◊ *To make* Petits Pains *(Little Breads), divide the dough into twelve pieces (instead of four), and shape each one into an oval loaf about 6 inches long.* Petits Pains *bake up a few minutes faster.*

MAKES 4 LOAVES

1½ packages active dry yeast
1 tablespoon honey
2 teaspoons salt
2 cups hot water (about 125°F., see page 9)

6 to 7 cups unbleached enriched white flour
1 to 2 tablespoons yellow cornmeal

In a large mixing bowl, combine the yeast, honey, and salt.

Add the hot water and stir well.

Add 2 cups of the flour and stir in well. \

With a wooden spoon, stir in another 3 cups of flour, ½ cup at a time, stirring each well. If the going gets too stiff for the spoon, work in the last cup with your hand.

Spread the sixth cup of flour on the kneading board, scrape the dough onto it, turn it over, and begin to knead.

Knead in as much of the final cup of flour as required to make a dough that is elastic, cohesive, and quite responsive when you poke it.

Continue to knead for about another 10 minutes, lightly dusting your hands or the board with flour if the dough sticks.

When the dough is ready (see Kneading, page 1), pour a tablespoon of oil into your scraped-out mixing bowl and put the dough in, and turn the dough to oil all sides.

Cover the bowl with a dry towel and set in a very warm, draft-free place to rise for about 1 hour, until the dough has at least doubled in volume, and passes the finger test (see page 6).

Grease two large cookie sheets and sprinkle with the yellow cornmeal, tapping each sheet to make a thin, even layer.

When the dough is sufficiently risen, make a fist and punch the dough down, then knead it briefly in the bowl to get rid of the larger bubbles.

In the bowl, cut the dough into four equal pieces.

Dust the kneading board with a little flour.

One at a time, starting in the middle, roll out each piece of dough with your hands into the traditional French "baguette" shape, about 1½ inches thick and fairly even.

Place two loaves on each cookie sheet, leaving room for spread.

Cover with dry towels and place in a warm, draft-free place to rise, for about half the time of that first rise.

Peek after about 10 minutes. If the loaves are spreading rather than rising, remove from any bottom heat, and allow to rise at room temperature (75°F. minimum). When the loaves are risen, they will look about twice as big as before.

Now, it is time to slash the loaves. With a single-edged razor or a very sharp knife, make three or four diagonal cuts equally spaced along the top of each loaf, cutting ⅛ to ¼ inch deep. Do not cut too deep or the bread will fall.

Mist the loaves well with tepid water.

Just before baking, place a cake pan on the bottom of the oven. Boil 2 cups of water and pour into the pan.

Starting in a cold oven set for 400°F., bake for 30 to 40 minutes, until the bottoms of the loaves are a deep golden brown and the bread tests done (see page 7).

During the baking, pull the loaves forward and spray twice more: after 10 minutes and then 5 minutes later.

When done, cool briefly on a wire rack.

If possible, serve the bread hot, tearing off chunks in the French manner.

$\frac{9}{4}$ $\frac{6}{4}$ 1½ tsp

+ a little

3 - ½ cup flour

1 cup hot H₂0

Italian Bread

Italian Bread is work. It is the most difficult kneading of any of the breads in this book, and it makes the driest dough. And yet it should rise without difficulty and bake up to a deliciously moist bread.

◇ *On a damp day, this dough will hold a full 9 cups of flour; on a dry day, be content with 8½ cups.*

◇ *We flatten this dough with a rolling pin and then roll it up into a spiral to improve its "web" (the pattern of air bubbles in the dough).*

◇ *As with French Bread, to help the crust get crisp, we spray the loaves with water, and put a pan of water in the bottom of the oven during baking to raise the humidity.*

◇ *If you want the crackled surface that is typical of Italian bread, cool the loaves in the breeze from an electric fan!*

◇ *For a more nutritious bread, ½ cup of wheat germ or bran can be substituted for ½ cup of flour (say, at cup 4).*

◇ *Or whole wheat flour can be substituted for up to half of the white flour. You will use less flour in total because the whole wheat is more absorbent, but the dough will take longer to rise.*

◇ *For an "adventure," substitute chicken soup for the hot water and 1 cup of soy flour for 1 cup white (at about cup 7). This makes a rich bread that toasts beautifully.*

◇ *For Parma Bread, add 6 tablespoons of grated Parmesan cheese to the dough. (See also Cresca, page 124.)*

◇ *For Pane di San Giuseppi (St. Joseph's Bread), add 6 table-spoons of anise seed after the hot water, and then shape the loaf to look like a patriarch's beard—or any other shape you please.*

◇ *For Bread Sticks, tear off walnut-sized pieces of the risen dough and roll into strips a little thinner than your pinky. Pinch the ends smooth and place on a greased baking sheet to rise for about half the time of the first rise. Brush with milk and sprinkle with sesame seeds, then bake at 350°F. for 12 to 15 minutes, or until golden brown. Eat one or two (or more) to make sure they are done. See also Whole Wheat Italian Bread Sticks, page 32.*

◊ *For Garlic Bread, add 2 tablespoons (or more!) of dried garlic flakes after the hot water.*

MAKES 3 LOAVES

2 packages active dry yeast
1 tablespoon honey
2 cups hot water (about 125°F., see page 9)
4 teaspoons salt

¼ cup olive oil
8 to 9 cups unbleached enriched white flour
¼ cup yellow cornmeal

Into a large mixing bowl, measure the yeast, honey, water, and salt, and stir until the salt is dissolved.

Add the olive oil and stir in.

Mix in the first 4 cups of flour, 1 cup at a time, stirring with a whisk; switch to a wooden spoon when the going gets too heavy for a whisk.

Stirring well between each new addition, mix in the next 2 cups of flour, ½ cup at a time.

Spread a ½ cup of flour on the kneading board, scrape the dough onto it, then spread another ½ cup on top. Knead this flour in.

Spread another cup of flour (number 8) over the board—this dough will take that cup and more—and knead it in well.

Knead in as much of the final ½ cup as you can force in.

This should be a very resistant dough. You have "enough" flour in when you can shape the dough into a ball, lean on it with your hand, and still have it want to stay a couple of inches thick.

When you have enough flour in, knead for another 5 to 10 minutes.

Pour a tablespoon of olive oil into your scraped-out mixing bowl, put the dough in, and turn the dough to oil all sides.

Cover the bowl with a dry towel and set in a warm, draft-free place to rise for about 1½ hours—or until it has doubled in volume and passes the finger test (see page 6).

Grease two large cookie sheets and sprinkle each with about 2 tablespoons of yellow cornmeal, tapping the sheets to get an even layer.

When the dough is risen, punch it down, turn it out onto your kneading board, then knead for a minute to get rid of the larger bubbles.

Divide the dough into three balls.

Flatten a ball with your rolling pin or by hand, into a rectangle about 10 by 12 inches.

Now, starting from the longer side of the rectangle, rolling as tightly as you can manage, without air spaces, roll the dough into a long, thin cigar shape, about 2 inches thick and long enough to stretch across your cookie sheet.

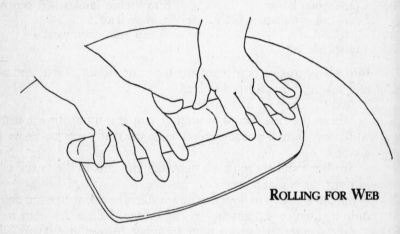

ROLLING FOR WEB

When the rolling is finished, pinch the seam closed and turn it down; pinch the ends closed and tuck them under. Place one loaf on one cookie sheet, and two loaves on the other, seam and tucked ends down.

With a single-edged razor or a very sharp knife, make three diagonal slashes, evenly spaced down the loaf, about ½ inch deep.

Mist the surface of the loaves with water until they are wet.

Cover with dry towels and set in a warm, draft-free place to rise for about half the time of the first rise. When risen, the slashes will gape wide.

When the loaves are almost risen, boil 2 cups of water. Place a cake pan in the bottom of the oven, and pour the boiling water into it.

Once again, give the loaves a good spraying.

Starting in a cold oven set for 375°F., bake the loaves for 30 to 40 minutes, or until the bread tests done (see page 7).

During the baking, pull the loaves forward and spray twice more: after 10 minutes and again after 15 minutes.

When done, cool on a wire rack (using the breeze of an electric fan to make the crust crackle).

If possible, serve the bread while it is still warm, when it's at its tastiest.

REFRIGERATOR-RISE BREADS

For some of our students this is the "basic" bread: it's the one their kids prefer because it looks the most like the commercial loaf they've been conditioned to by ads.

Refrigerator-Rise Bread is also a favorite with people on a tight schedule. It can be kneaded and shaped the night before, kept in the refrigerator (where it rises—hence, the name), and in the morning popped into the oven and baked to serve hot with breakfast. Or it can be baked for dinner, if you take it from refrigerator to oven as soon as you come home from work.

These are moist doughs, made with oil. Whatever other changes you try, don't leave out the oil, because it is the oil that allows them ro rise so well in the refrigerator.

These breads need at least 5 hours to rise and should not be left for more than 24 hours. Less than 5 hours means they don't get enough rise. More than 24 hours and they can collapse, which means that the bread must be rekneaded and allowed to rise again.

◊ *Refrigerator-rise breads have a coarser web (the pattern of air bubbles in the dough) than many of our breads because they have only that one refrigerator rise: there is no first rise in a bowl, and then a kneading down and a second rise, which makes for a finer web.*

◊ *When you put the loaves in the refrigerator, cover them with oiled plastic wrap or waxed paper. An unoiled covering can stick to the dough when you try to remove it, causing the bread to collapse.*

◊ *Whole wheat flour can be substituted for up to half of the white. Remember, whole wheat is more absorbent and you'll wind up using less total flour.*

◊ *If you are baking for kids, whole milk can be substituted for the nonfat. Or use "supermilk"—2 cups of whole milk plus ⅔ cup of instant nonfat milk powder.*

◊ *For a treat, ½ cup of unsulfured raisins or as much as ¾ cup of sesame seeds or sunflower seeds can be kneaded in either of the refrigerator-rise breads when shaping the loaves.*

Wheat Germ Refrigerator-Rise Bread

MAKES 3 LOAVES IN 8½-INCH PANS

2 packages active dry yeast
2 tablespoons honey
1 tablespoon salt
2 cups very warm nonfat milk (about 115°F., see page 9)
½ cup unsaturated oil

4 cups unbleached enriched white flour
1 cup wheat germ
1 to 2 cups unbleached enriched white flour (additional)

In a large mixing bowl, combine the yeast, honey, salt, and milk, and stir well.

Mix in the oil.

Beating each cup in well with a wooden spoon, add the first 4 cups of flour, 1 cup at a time.

Beat in the wheat germ.

Spread 1 cup of flour on the kneading board, scrape the moist dough over it, turn the dough over, and work in this flour.

Knead in as much of an additional ½ cup or so as required to make soft, but not sticky, dough. Don't force in a lot of flour. Stop adding flour (except for dustings) when the dough can be handled without sticking.

Knead for an additional 10 minutes.

Grease well three 8½-inch loaf pans.

Cut the dough into three pieces, and shape each piece into a small loaf giving the "karate chop" described on page 27 if you want smooth end slices.

Put the loaves into pans and cover each pan *loosely* with plastic wrap.

Place in your refrigerator so that the pans are not touching, and with room above for rise.

Allow to rise for a minimum of 5 and a maximum of 24 hours.

Remove from the refrigerator and take off the plastic carefully. Do not touch the dough.

Starting in a cold oven set at 350°F., bake for about 50 minutes, or until the tops are dark brown and the loaves test done (see page 7).

Cool on a wire rack, and serve warm.

Oatmeal Refrigerator-Rise Bread

This bread is a good keeper, staying fresh days longer than you would expect.

◊ *The recipe calls for 5 to 5½ cups of flour, but the amount of flour will depend on your brand of oatmeal (different processing techniques make for different absorptions).*

◊ *Do not use instant oatmeal—the recipe will work with quick oats and rolled oats, but not instant.*

MAKES 3 LOAVES IN 8½-INCH PANS

1½ cups boiling water
1½ cups oatmeal
⅓ cup unsaturated oil
⅓ cup honey
2 packages active dry yeast
1 tablespoon salt

1 cup yogurt (or buttermilk)
4 cups unbleached enriched white flour
¼ cup wheat germ
1 to 1½ cups unbleached enriched white flour (additional)

In a large bowl, pour the boiling water over the oatmeal and stir until everything is wet.

Measure in the oil, then the honey, and stir in well. Allow to cool until just moderately hot to the touch.

Stir in the yeast, then the salt and yogurt. Mix well.

Add the 4 cups of flour, 1 cup at a time, stirring each cup in well with a wooden spoon.

Mix the wheat germ in well.

Pour 1 cup of the additional flour on the kneading board, scrape the dough onto it, turn it over, then gently begin to work this flour in. This is a sticky dough, but resist the temptation to knead in every last bit of flour that you can. Clean your hands of dough and dust them with flour frequently, using as much of the last ½ cup as required.

When the dough pretty much stops sticking, it has enough flour. Now knead for an additional 10 minutes.

Grease well three 8½-inch loaf pans.

Divide the dough into thirds and shape three loaves. Finish the ends of the loaves with a "karate chop" (see page 27).

Put the loaves into the pans, and cover each pan loosely with a piece of oiled plastic. Place in the refrigerator so that the pans are not touching, and with room above for the rise.

Allow to rise for at least 5 hours and no more than 24 hours.

Remove from the refrigerator and carefully take off the plastic wrap. Do not touch the dough. Starting in a cold oven, set at 375° to 400°F., bake for about 40 minutes, or until the loaves test done (see page 7).

Cool on a wire rack, and serve warm.

SPIRAL BREADS

Here is a bread that can keep you and your family interested day after day, because, like Cleopatra (a noted Egyptian bread baker), custom cannot stale its infinite variety.

It is called spiral bread because the dough is rolled out to ¼ inch thick, spread with various fillings, and then rolled up tightly, so when the baked loaf is sliced, a spiral is visible.

There is virtually no limit to the variations you can create with this bread. Herb fillings give you a bread to complement any main course; ground shrimp or meat give you a bread that can be a main course in itself; sweet fillings give you a dessert bread.

◊ *Testing can be a problem with Dessert Spirals and Cheese-Herb Spirals. Cheese, honey, or jam stay liquid after the dough is done, and so a knife test (see page 7) may show something sticking to the knife. Do examine the knife closely and wipe off what is on the blade. Generally, melted cheese and honey and jam wipe off easily while unbaked dough does not.*

◊ *Spiral bread dough also makes excellent rolls—see Kaiser Rolls (page 87) and Knot Rolls (page 90).*

◊ *If you wish to bake only one spiral, refrigerate or freeze two thirds of the dough (see page 232) to use later for bread or rolls.*

Herb Fillings

◊ With herb fillings, we usually brush the rolled-out dough with melted butter before sprinkling with filling, to help the separate swirls of the spiral stand out after baking. But the buttering may be omitted if you wish to lower the butterfat and calories.

◊ Our favorite herb filling uses grated Parmesan cheese (enough to cover the buttered dough with a thin layer), oregano, and fennel seed. But any other combination that appeals is also appropriate, for instance: grated cheddar and dill and parsley; grated Swiss and fresh dillweed; turmeric and curry powder; chili and cumin powder.

◊ In creating your combinations, use 2 tablespoons of a fresh herb, 1 tablespoon of a dried herb, 2 teaspoons of a seed, and about ¼ cup of a grated cheese per loaf.

◊ For Cheese-Herb Spiral, butter the outside and sprinkle with more cheese before rising the loaves.

Sweet Fillings

Here is where the compliments get extravagant.

◊ No buttering of the rolled-out dough is required for most of these fillings since they are moist.

◊ Cinnamon and honey is a simple and marvelously delicious filling: For the three loaves, mix 4 teaspoons of cinnamon with ¾ cup of honey. Brush this on the rolled-out dough and roll it up to make a Cinnamon Spiral.

◊ Or, substitute maple syrup for the honey.

◊ Or, butter the dough and sprinkle with maple sugar or date sugar.

◊ Or, mix 4 teaspoons of carob powder with ½ cup of honey for a chocolatey taste without chocolate's drawbacks. Add some ground nuts if you like.

◊ For a very simple filling, brush on a thin layer of a sugarless jam.

◊ For Cinnamon Spirals, spray the outside with a little water and dust on some more cinnamon before rising the loaves.

Main-Course Fillings

◊ Butter the rolled-out dough, and sprinkle on a few raw ground shrimp and 2 teaspoons of fennel seed per loaf.

◊ Or, with no butter, try raw chopped beef (sprinkled thin) with a little chili powder.

◊ Or, butter the dough and spread on ground cooked chick-peas or kidney beans with cumin seeds, for a meatless main course.

◊ You must refrigerate any leftovers from these Main Course Breads.

Spiral Bread

MAKES 3 LOAVES IN 8½-INCH PANS, OR 3 RINGS

The Dough:

2 packages active dry yeast
2 teaspoons salt
2 tablespoons honey
2 cups hot water (about 125°F., see page 9)

½ cup nonfat milk powder
¼ cup unsaturated oil
1 cup wheat germ
5 to 6 cups unbleached enriched white flour

The Filling:

whatever appeals (see Herb, Sweet, and Main-Course Fillings, above)

In a large bowl, combine the yeast, salt, honey, and water, and stir well.

Stir in the milk powder, then the oil.

Mix in the wheat germ.

With a whisk, beat in the first 4 cups of flour, 1 cup at a time, changing to a wooden spoon when the going gets tough.

Spread a fifth cup of flour over the kneading board, scrape the dough onto it, turn the dough over, and gently work this flour in.

Knead in as much of another cup of flour as required to make the dough stop sticking. After that, just dust your hands and the surfaces lightly, and knead for a brisk 5 minutes, until those characteristic light wrinkles appear.

When kneaded (see page 1), pour about a tablespoon of oil into your scraped-out mixing bowl, put in the dough, then turn the dough over to oil all sides. Cover and put to rise in a warm, draft-free place for about 1 hour, until the dough is doubled in volume and tests risen (see page 5).

When the dough is risen, punch it down in the bowl and knead for a minute to get rid of the larger bubbles.

Divide the dough into three equal pieces and shape into balls.

Sprinkle a thin layer of flour onto the kneading board before rolling the dough out, and dust the board and the rolling pin lightly every time you turn the dough.

Place a ball of dough on the floured board and begin to flatten it by pressing and pushing it with your hand. Then turn the dough and switch to the floured rolling pin. Turning frequently (and dusting), roll into a rectangle about 8 by 12 inches and ¼ inch thick.

Now, turn the dough over a final time and put on your filling, following the directions for fillings, above.

When the filling is on, roll the dough up tightly. Roll from the short side to make a loaf for an 8½-inch loaf pan; or from the long side to make in a ring mold. The secret of a successful spiral is to roll tightly.

Grease well three loaf pans or ring molds.

Wet your fingers and pinch the seams and ends closed, then place seam down in the loaf pan. Or, for a ring mold, place in the mold and then pinch the ends together. Repeat for the other two loaves.

Cover with a dry towel and put in a warm, draft-free place to rise for about ½ hour, until the loaf has swelled appreciably, but not doubled.

Starting in a cold oven, bake at about 360°F. for 30 to 40 minutes, or until the loaf tests done (see page 7).

Cool on a wire rack, and serve warm.

～ 4 ～

Quick-Rising Breads

THE yeasts used in "quick-rising breads" are a new discovery. They are as much an advance over active dry yeasts as active dry yeasts were over cake yeasts in the 1940s. And yet, all three types of yeast are still on the market.

Both of the two major yeast producers, Fleischmann's and Red Star, sell quick-rising yeasts, and they each say that these yeasts are different strains from active dry yeasts—and that the two brands are different from each other as well.

As far as you, the bread baker, are concerned, the main difference between active dry yeasts and quick-rising yeasts is the rising time: quick-rising yeasts will rise bread in about half the time of active dry yeasts. We find no detectable difference in flavor, or the amount of rise, or the quality of the bread produced.

There *is* a difference, however, in the way the two types of yeast are handled. Active dry yeasts should be mixed with a liquid to begin with. Quick-rising yeasts should be mixed with the flour, to which hot liquid is then added.

Red Star calls its product "Quick-Rise." It is intended to be used either directly mixed with the flour, or substituted for the yeast in an active-dry yeast recipe ("started" by mixing in water). We have tried the substitution, and it works very well.

Fleischmann's "RapidRise" yeast is intended only for mixing with the flour—Fleischmann's has told us that it will not react properly if dissolved in water first.

Our quick-rising recipes work with either brand of quick-rising yeast.

We have given you a wide selection of quick-rising breads and rolls here, but you can adapt many of the yeast-bread recipes in this book to the quick-rising method (see page 16).

Quick-Rising French Bread

Here is a true French bread: crusty, chewy, and *très vite*.

◊ *We spray the loaves with water and put a pan of water in the oven during baking to make that marvelous French bread crust.*
◊ *The cornmeal on the baking sheet gives the loaf bottoms added crunch—but don't let a lack of cornmeal keep you from baking these excellent baguettes.*

MAKES 2 LOAVES

2 cups unbleached enriched white flour
1 package quick-rising yeast
1 teaspoon salt
1½ cups hot water (about 125°F., see page 9)

¼ cup wheat germ
¼ cup bran
1¾ to 2 cups unbleached enriched white flour (additional)
2 tablespoons yellow cornmeal

In a large bowl, mix together the 2 cups of flour, and the yeast and salt.

Add the hot water and mix until all the flour is wet.

Beat with an electric beater for 5 minutes (about 10 minutes by whisk), until a lot of elasticity is developed.

Add the wheat germ and bran, and mix in until wet.

Using a wooden spoon, beat in 1 cup of the additional flour, ½ cup at a time.

Sprinkle ¼ cup of flour on the kneading board, scrape the batter onto the flour, sprinkle another ¼ cup over the top, and begin to knead gently.

Knead for a total of about 10 minutes, kneading in as much of an additional ½ cup of flour as required to make a very elastic but still moist dough. (This makes a total of about 4 cups of flour.)

Pour a teaspoon of oil into the bottom of the scraped-out mixing bowl, put in the dough ball, and turn to oil all sides.

Set the dough to rise, with a dry towel, covered in a very warm, draft-free place, for about 40 minutes, or until it has more than doubled. Finger-test for sufficient rise (see page 6).

When the dough has risen, knead briefly and gently in the bowl to get it down to its original size, then cut it in half.

Preheat your oven to 400°F., and set a cake pan filled with hot water on the bottom shelf.

Grease a large baking sheet and sprinkle it with the cornmeal, tapping the sheet to make a thin, even layer.

Shape each half of the dough into a thin loaf about a foot long, and place on the greased and cornmeal-coated sheet, leaving some room between for spread.

Cover with a dry towel and let rise at room temperature (70°F. minimum) for 20 to 25 minutes, or until about doubled in width.

When the loaves have risen, spray them well with tepid water. With a single-edged razor or a very sharp knife, make three diagonal slashes equally spaced a couple of inches apart along the top of each loaf, cutting to a depth of only ⅛ inch. Do not cut too deep or the bread will fall.

Bake for 30 minutes, or until the loaves are a deep gold and test done (see page 7).

Cool briefly on a wire rack, and serve hot.

Quick-Rising High-Fiber Bread

This is a heavy bread—no surprise in a recipe that is about 20 percent bran—but it is delicious, and loaded with fiber. The loaves are small, but sliced thin the bread makes excellent sandwiches.

◊ *To keep this bread moist, work in as little of the last flour as you can and still have a dough that is not sticky. Try kneading it in a large enamel or ceramic bowl, or on a marble board: these surfaces will demand less flour than a wooden board.*

MAKES 2 LOAVES IN 7½-INCH PANS

1 cup bran
4 cups whole wheat flour
2 packages quick-rising yeast
1 teaspoon salt
½ cup unsulfured raisins

½ cup honey
1½ cups water
½ to 1 cup whole wheat flour (additional)

In a large bowl, combine the bran, the 4 cups of flour, and the yeast, salt, and raisins, and stir until well mixed.

Combine the honey and water in a saucepan, and heat to about 125°F.—quite hot but not burning (use a candy thermometer if you want to check it).

Add the honey and water to the bowl and mix well, until the batter begins to show some cohesion and a tendency to pull away from the sides of the bowl.

Put a couple of tablespoons of the additional flour onto the kneading board, scrape the batter onto it, sprinkle the top with another 2 tablespoons of flour, and begin to knead. (Or, add the flour to the bowl and knead there.)

Knead for 7 to 10 minutes (dusting your hands with as much of the remaining ½ cup as necessary) until the dough is springy and has a smooth outside texture.

Pour a teaspoon of oil into the bottom of the scraped-out mixing bowl, put in the dough and turn it to oil all sides. Then set it to rise, covered with a warm, wet towel in a warm, draft-free place for 45 to 50 minutes.

Grease two 7½-inch pans. When the dough has about doubled and passes the finger test (page 6), divide it in half and put each half into a pan, poking the dough until it fills the corners and is more or less level.

Cover each loaf with a warm, wet towel and set to rise in a warm place, for 20 to 25 minutes, until the dough fills the pans.

Starting in a cold oven set at 375°F., bake for about 40 minutes, until the bread tests done (see page 7).

Turn the loaves out of the pans, and cool on a wire rack.

Quick-Rising Herb Sandwich Bread

Here is a nutritious and flavorful bread that makes an excellent sandwich—it even slices thin. The herbs are intended to supplement—not overpower—a sandwich filling.

This recipe has so much bran and wheat germ that it is nutritionally superior to plain whole wheat bread.

◊ Many grocers carry fresh parsley and dill year-round. Pots of chives can be grown on sunny windowsills.
◊ For more kick, add a tablespoon of chopped fresh rosemary.
◊ Or, substitute chopped fresh basil for the parsley.

MAKES 2 LARGE LOAVES IN 9½-INCH PANS

4 cups unbleached enriched white flour
2 packages quick-rising yeast
1 tablespoon salt
3 cups hot nonfat milk (about 125°F, see page 9)
3 large eggs, at room temperature
¼ cup finely chopped fresh parsley
¼ cup finely chopped fresh dill
¼ cup finely chopped fresh chives
2 large cloves garlic, finely chopped
1 cup wheat germ
1 cup bran
3 cups unbleached enriched white flour (additional)

Measure the 4 cups of flour into a large bowl, sprinkle the yeast and salt over the top, then stir until mixed.

Stir in the milk, break in the eggs, and beat the mixture with an electric mixer for about 5 minutes (or about 10 minutes by hand with a whisk), until elastic.

Stir in the herbs, mixing well.

Mix in the wheat germ and bran.

Add 1 cup of the additional flour to the bowl, and mix with a wooden spoon until all the flour is wet.

Pour a cup of flour over the kneading board, scrape the dough onto the flour, turn it over with a scraper, and begin to knead gently.

Knead for about 10 or 12 minutes until you have kneaded in an additional (the seventh) cup of flour. Knead until the dough is quite springy and medium-dry (see Kneading, page 1).

Pour about 1 tablespoon of oil into the bottom of the scraped-out mixing bowl, put in the dough, and turn it to oil all sides.

Set the dough to rise, covered with a dry towel, in a very warm, draft-free place, for about ¾ hour, or until the dough has at least doubled in volume and passes the finger test (page 6).

Grease two 9½ × 5½-inch loaf pans.

When risen, knead the dough briefly in the bowl to get it back to its original size, and to get rid of the larger bubbles.

Divide the dough in half, shape each half into an oval, and put into the pans. The dough should half-fill the pans.

Cover each loaf with a dry towel and set to rise again for 20 to 25 minutes, or until the dough fills the pans.

Starting in a cold oven set for 375°F., bake for about 40 minutes, until the bottoms are golden and the loaves test done (see page 7).

Turn the loaves out of the pans and cool on a wire rack.

Quick-Rising Coffee Cake or Sweet Rolls

Here is a delicious cinnamon-nut coffee cake that needs only three quarters of an hour's total rise. We got this recipe from a European-born cook whose *schnecken* was *wunderbar*. The original recipe contained four times as much butter before we tampered with it, but we think you'll find our lower cholesterol version delicious.

◊ *Don't leave out the lemon rind: it gives a "brightness" to the flavor of the dough.*
◊ *If you don't mind the extra calories and sugar, sprinkle another ¼ cup of brown sugar into the bottom of the buttered pan before you put in the pieces. It makes the bottom magic.*
◊ *If you want to save a few fat calories, melt only 3 tablespoons of butter, and do not butter the top.*

MAKES 1 9-INCH ROUND COFFEE CAKE

The Dough:

3¼ cups unbleached enriched white flour
¼ cup wheat germ
grated zest of 1 lemon
1 package quick-rising yeast

¾ cup nonfat milk
¼ cup corn oil
¼ cup honey
½ cup unsulfured raisins
2 large eggs, at room temperature

The Filling:

4 tablespoons sweet butter
½ cup chopped walnuts (medium-fine)

1 tablespoon ground cinnamon
½ cup brown sugar

Set aside ¾ cup of the flour.

In a large mixing bowl, combine the rest of the flour with the wheat germ, zest, and yeast. Stir with a whisk until the mixture is uniform.

In a saucepan, heat the milk, oil, and honey to about 125°F.

Pour the hot liquid over the dry ingredients, then beat in with an electric beater, or by hand with a whisk.

Add the raisins.

Break the eggs into the oil-and-honey measuring cup and whisk briefly. Add to the batter and work in.

Beat or whisk for a few minutes, until the batter is uniform and shows elasticity when you pull the beater from the batter.

Sprinkle about a ¼ cup of the reserved flour onto your kneading board and turn out the batter onto it, scraping the bowl well.

Knead for only a few minutes, working in most of the remaining flour, but keeping a very soft, elastic dough.

Pour a tablespoon of oil into the scraped-out mixing bowl, drop in the dough, and turn it to oil all sides.

Cover with a dry towel and set in a very warm, draft-free place to rise for about 30 minutes, or until the dough seems to have doubled and it passes the finger test (see page 6).

Meanwhile, melt (don't brown) the butter in a saucepan and reserve.

Prepare the filling: Mix the walnuts, cinnamon, and brown sugar and set aside.

Grease a 9-inch round cake pan, and set it aside.

Sprinkle a bit more flour on the kneading board and a rolling pin, and turn out the dough.

Knead gently and briefly to get out the air.

Using as little flour as possible, shape the dough into a cube and begin to roll it out. You want to wind up with a rectangular slab of dough, about 10 by 15 inches, with square corners. (To get square corners, cut off excess dough from the rounded sides and pinch it onto the corners.)

Turn the dough over a couple of times as you roll it out, dusting the board lightly each time.

When you have rolled out and squared off the dough, spread about three quarters of the melted butter over the top of the dough slab with a pastry brush.

Sprinkle the nut filling over the buttered dough, right out to the edges.

Now, roll up the dough, from the long side, into a moderately tight cylinder and pinch the long edge closed.

With a sharp knife, cut the roll in half, and then cut each half in half—giving you four pieces. Then cut each quarter into equal thirds—yielding a grand total of twelve pieces.

Place each piece into the cake pan, with one of the cut sides showing. Brush the tops with the leftover melted butter.

Cover with a dry towel and set to rise in a warm place for only 15 minutes.

Preheat your oven to 350°F.

Bake for about 30 minutes, or until the cake is a lovely golden brown and well risen, and tests done with a sharp knife (see page 7).

Serve hot or cooled, either as slices or pulled apart into individual sweet rolls.

Quick-Rising Tea Ring or Twists

Cardamom, which flavors this dough, is the characteristic flavor of Danish pastry—but it is difficult to make Danish pastry without using lots of butter. So we make this no-butter Danish-style bread instead. With its spice and its nuts, it is superdelicious.

◊ *We give this dough an extra rise in the bowl to make a finer texture.*

MAKES 2 LARGE RINGS, OR 32 TWISTS (OR 1 RING AND 16 TWISTS)

The Dough:

2 cups unbleached enriched white flour
2 packages quick-rising yeast
1 teaspoon salt
1 cup hot nonfat milk (about 125°F., see page 9)
¾ cup unsaturated oil, at room temperature
1 cup honey, at room temperature

3 large eggs, at room temperature
1 tablespoon ground cardamom
¼ cup wheat germ
¼ cup bran
5 cups unbleached enriched white flour (additional)
1 cup filberts, ground fine (grinds to 1½ cups)

The Glaze:

1 large egg

1 tablespoon water

In a large bowl, combine the 2 cups of flour, the yeast, and the salt, and mix well.

Stir in the milk, then the oil and honey. Beat for 5 minutes with an electric mixer (or about 10 minutes by whisk) to develop the elasticity.

Beat in the eggs, cardamom, wheat germ, and bran.

Switch over to a wooden spoon, and beat in 4 cups of the additional flour, 1 cup at a time.

Sprinkle ¼ cup of flour onto your kneading board, scrape the dough onto it, sprinkle another ¼ cup of flour over the top, and begin to knead. Knead for about 8 minutes, working in as much of the remaining ½ cup of flour as required, until you reach a total of about 7 cups. The dough should wind up satiny but not sticky; firm but not stiff.

Pour 1 tablespoon of oil into the scraped-out mixing bowl, drop in the dough, and turn it to oil all sides.

Cover with a dry towel and set to rise in a very warm, draft-free place, until the dough has doubled in volume and passed the finger test (page 6)—about 1 hour.

When risen, punch the dough down, cover with the towel again, and set back in the same place to rise again for about 30 minutes.

When re-risen, punch down in the bowl again, flour the kneading board lightly, and turn out the dough.

With your hands or a rolling pin, roll the dough out to a large, thin rectangle, then sprinkle with about ¼ cup of the ground nuts.

Fold this rectangle into thirds, and roll it out again to its original size. Sprinkle with another ¼ cup of nuts, and fold and roll it again. Repeat this a third time, keeping the remaining nuts (½ to ¾ cup) for the glaze.

Grease two large cookie sheets, and preheat your oven to 375°F. Divide the dough in half.

To make a ring, roll out one half to a cylinder about 24 inches long, and then squeeze the last few inches of each end of the cylinder to half its thickness and twice its length (see illustration). Place the dough on one cookie sheet, bringing the thick parts of the dough around in a circle, and twisting the thinner parts of the dough together in a simple over and under to close the ring. Make a second ring with the other half of the dough.

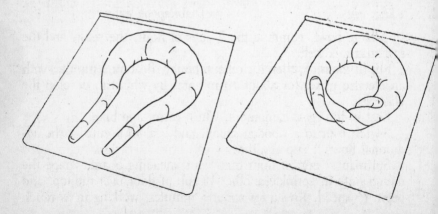

To make twists, roll half of the dough out to a ¼-inch slab about 12 by 4½ or 5 inches. Cut the dough into four strips 12 inches long, and then cut each strip into four equal pieces. Put the pieces on a greased baking sheet. Place a finger on the center of each piece, and twist the strip so that one half is "face down." Repeat with the remaining dough for 32 twists.

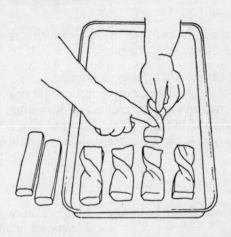

Cover the trays with dry towels and set to rise at room temperature (70°F. minimum) for about 30 minutes, or until the rings or twists are somewhat risen.

To glaze the twists or rings: Whisk an egg and a tablespoon of water together, and brush well over all the exposed surfaces with a pastry brush. Sprinkle the tops and sides generously with the remaining ground nuts.

Bake the rings for 25 to 30 minutes, the twists for about 15 minutes. Test for doneness (see page 7).

Cool on a wire rack—these are wonderful hot, but also excellent at room temperature.

Quick-Rising Three-Seed Round Rye

This is a vibrantly tasty rye bread, grand for sandwiches, or just toasted and eaten with your meal.

◇ *Make certain that the seeds are fresh.*
◇ *A lot of vigorous kneading is required for this bread because rye flour contains so little gluten (see Kneading, page 1).*
◇ *If you want to make this a four-seed bread, sprinkle Russian caraway over the egg glaze instead of caraway.*

MAKES 2 LOAVES

The Dough:

3 cups unbleached enriched white flour
2 packages quick-rising yeast
1 teaspoon salt
2 cups hot nonfat milk (about 125°F., see page 9)

1 tablespoon caraway seeds
2 teaspoons poppy seeds
1 tablespoon sesame seeds
2 cups rye flour
2 tablespoons yellow cornmeal

The Glaze:

1 large egg
1 tablespoon water

2 teaspoons caraway seeds (additional)

Measure the white flour, yeast, and salt into a large mixing bowl.

Add the milk, and beat for 5 minutes with an electric mixer (or about 10 minutes by hand), until the batter is quite elastic.

Mix in the caraway, poppy, and sesame seeds.

With a wooden spoon, stir in about 1 cup of the rye flour.

Sprinkle about a ½ cup of rye flour on the kneading board, scrape the batter onto it, turn it over, and begin to work in the flour.

Adding the rest of the rye flour as needed, knead briskly for about 12 minutes, or until the dough is elastic and fairly dry.

Pour about 1 tablespoon of oil into the scraped-out mixing bowl, put in the dough, and turn it to oil all surfaces.

Cover with a warm, wet towel, and set to rise in a warm, draft-free place for about 40 minutes, or until the dough is well risen and has passed the finger test (page 6).

When risen, punch the dough down and knead it gently and briefly in the bowl. Then cut it in half.

Preheat your oven to 375°F.

Grease two baking sheets, and sprinkle each with a tablespoon of cornmeal, tapping the sheets to make a thin, even layer.

Shape each half of the dough into a ball, and place on separate sheets.

Cover, and put to rise in *gentle* warmth (no more than 80°F.) for about 25 minutes, or until well risen. The loaves will flatten slightly as they spread.

To glaze the loaves: Beat the egg with a tablespoon of water, and brush onto the loaves with a pastry brush, covering the surfaces thinly. Sprinkle each loaf with about 1 teaspoon of caraway seeds.

Bake for about 40 minutes, or until the loaves test done (see page 7).

Cool on a wire rack and serve warm.

Quick-Rising Cheese Braid

This is a beautiful bread—to see and to taste.

◇ *Make certain the cheese is sharp to extra-sharp cheddar, and don't skimp on it.*
◇ *Resist any temptation to make this bread with all unbleached enriched white flour: The look of the bread demands some whole wheat.*
◇ *Do not force more flour in than you have to. The dough must be stiff enough to hold its shape as it rises, and dry enough to roll out without additional flour, but not so stiff and dry as to bake up dense and low.*

MAKES 2 LOAVES

4 cups unbleached enriched white flour
2 packages quick-rising yeast
1 teaspoon salt
1 tablespoon caraway seeds
2½ cups hot nonfat milk (about 125°F., see page 9)

¼ cup honey
¾ pound extra-sharp cheddar cheese, grated (grates to 3 to 4 cups)
3 to 3½ cups whole wheat flour

In a large mixing bowl, stir together the white flour, yeast, salt, and caraway seeds.

In a separate bowl, mix together the milk and honey, and stir until the honey is dissolved.

Pour this mixture into the flour bowl, and mix until all the dry ingredients are wet.

Beat for about 5 minutes with an electric mixer (or about 10 minutes by hand), until the batter is quite elastic.

Stir in the grated cheese, then 1 cup of the whole wheat flour.

Pour ½ cup of whole wheat onto the kneading board, scrape the batter onto it, sprinkle more flour on top, turn the batter, and begin to knead.

Knead for about 8 to 10 minutes, working in about 1¼ to 1¾

cups more of whole wheat flour (making a total of about 3 to 3½ cups of whole wheat flour), until the flour no longer sticks and the dough is smooth, elastic, and cohesive.

Pour a tablespoon of oil into the scraped-out mixing bowl, put in the dough, and turn a few times to oil all sides.

Set to rise, covered with a dry towel, in a warm, draft-free place, for about 40 minutes, or until the dough has doubled or more, and it passes the finger test (page 6).

When risen, knead down gently in the bowl.

Grease two large baking sheets.

Cut the dough in half, then cut each half into three equal parts. Roll these pieces out to ropes about 1 inch thick and 16 inches long.

Place the three ropes alongside one another and, starting in the middle (see A, page 66), braid to one end, then turn the board or the dough and braid underhand down to the other end. (See B, page 66). Braiding this way makes a more symmetrical loaf.

When all braided, tuck both ends under and pinch closed—the ends must not open in the rising or baking. Transfer the braid to the baking sheet. Repeat with the other three ropes.

Each finished braid will be about 10 by 4 inches.

Cover each braid with a dry towel and allow to rise at room temperature (about 70°F.) for about a ½ hour, or until quite well risen.

Meanwhile, preheat your oven to 350°F.

Bake for about 30 minutes, or until the tops have browned and the bottoms are dark brown. Test for doneness with a toothpick inserted into the thickest joint (see page 7).

Cool briefly on a wire rack, but serve hot, torn apart.

Quick-Rising Braided Cheese Rolls

With very little more labor than it took for the Cheese Braid, these come to the table as impressive braided rolls.

MAKES 24 ROLLS

1 recipe Quick-Rising Cheese Braid
(page 64)

Mix the dough for Cheese Braid as described on page 64, continuing right through the first rise.

Preheat the oven to 375°F., and grease two large baking sheets.

Punch down the dough, and knead it in the bowl gently and briefly. Cut the dough into equal quarters.

Place one quarter on the board and cut into three equal pieces.

Roll each piece out to about ½ inch thick, and as long as you can make them.

Place the rolled ropes side by side, touching, and starting in the middle, braid overhand down to one end. Turn, and braid underhand down to the other end. Tuck the ends under and pinch closed.

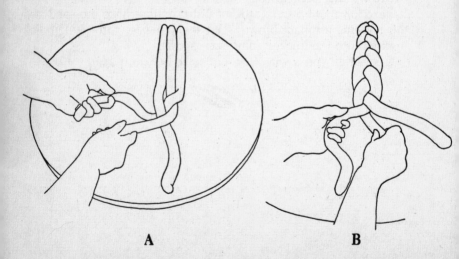

A   B

With a knife, cut each braid into six equal rolls, and place on a baking sheet, leaving ample room for rise and spread. Repeat with the next quarter of the dough, and place on this same sheet.

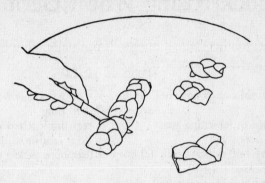

Repeat with the next two quarters, placing the rolls on the second sheet.

Cover with a dry towel, and set to rise at room temperature (70°F., minimum) for about 20 minutes, or until almost doubled.

Bake for about 20 to 22 minutes, or until the bottoms are browned and the rolls test done with a toothpick (see page 7).

Cool briefly on a wire rack, but serve hot.

Quick-Rising Wheat Germ Rolls

Call these either large dinner rolls or small club rolls.

MAKES 12 ROLLS

2 cups unbleached enriched white flour

1 package quick-rising yeast

1½ teaspoons salt

1½ cups hot nonfat milk (about 125°F., see page 9)

½ cup unbleached enriched white flour (additional)

½ cup wheat germ

¼ cup bran

1 cup unbleached enriched white flour (additional)

4 teaspoons yellow cornmeal

Into a large bowl, measure the 2 cups of flour, the yeast, and the salt, and mix.

Add the milk and stir in well. Beat about 5 minutes with an electric beater (or about 10 minutes by hand), until the batter is quite elastic.

Stir in an additional ½ cup of flour. When all wet, stir in the wheat germ and bran.

Sprinkle ¼ cup of the additional flour onto the kneading board, scrape the batter onto it, then sprinkle another ¼ cup of flour over it. Turn the batter over and work in this flour.

Knead for 6 to 8 minutes, working in a final ¾ of a cup to 1 cup of flour (making a total of 3¾ to 4 cups of flour). The dough should be fairly dry and stiff—but not rigid.

Measure about 1 tablespoon of oil into the scraped-out mixing bowl, put in the dough, and turn it to oil all surfaces.

Put into a warm, draft-free place to rise, covered with a dry towel, for about 35 minutes—until about doubled. It should easily pass the finger test (see page 6).

When risen, punch the dough down and knead gently in the bowl to remove the larger bubbles.

Grease a large baking pan with sides, and scatter the cornmeal over the surface. (Hit the side of the pan with your hand to even the sprinkling.)

Divide the dough into four roughly equal pieces. One at a time, roll each piece out to about a foot, as evenly as you can, then cut each into three pieces. Even out the size and shape, and place on the pan. Turn each roll over once to get some cornmeal on the top, then return to its original position.

Preheat your oven to 400°F.

Set to rise, covered with a dry towel, in a warm place. Check after 10 minutes of rising. If the rolls are spreading instead of rising, remove from the warm place, and finish the rise at room temperature (about 70°F.), covered.

Bake for about 18 minutes, or until the tops are lightly browned and the bottoms are well browned.

Test one or two for doneness with a toothpick (see page 7).

Cool briefly on a wire rack and serve warm.

Quick-Rising Whole Wheat Figure-Eight Squash Rolls

We make these into figure-eights by joining two balls of dough, but you can bake them in any shape you wish, using the roll techniques described in Chapter 5.

Cooked butternut squash is high in vitamin A—something you don't usually get much of in bread.

MAKES ABOUT 18 ROLLS

3 cups whole wheat flour
½ teaspoon salt
½ rounded teaspoon ground cloves
1 package quick-rising yeast
¼ cup unsaturated oil
½ cup nonfat milk

½ cup honey
¾ cup cooked butternut squash, mashed
1 large egg, at room temperature
¾ to 1 cup whole wheat flour (additional)

Into a large bowl measure the 3 cups of flour, the salt, cloves, and yeast, and stir until fairly uniform.

Into a 2-cup measure pour the oil, milk, honey, and squash. Put this mixture into a saucepan and heat to about 125°F. (see page 9). Add it to the flour mixture and stir well with a wooden spoon.

Beat the mixture for a few minutes with an electric mixer (or about 6 minutes by hand), then, when the batter is elastic, stir in ½ cup of the additional flour.

Spread ¼ cup of flour on the kneading board, scrape the batter onto it, and sprinkle more flour on top. Work in this flour, then knead, adding as much of the remaining ½ cup of flour as required, for about 5 minutes. (This makes a total of 3¾ to 4 cups of flour.) Don't make the dough too dry.

Pour a teaspoon of oil into the scraped-out mixing bowl, put in the dough and turn to oil all sides. Cover with a warm, wet towel and set to rise in a warm, draft-free place for about 45 minutes, or until the finger test shows it to be risen (see page 6).

Knead the dough briefly in the bowl to get rid of the large bubbles. Grease a large cookie sheet.

Pull off a walnut-sized lump of dough and gently roll into a ball, then place on the cookie sheet. Make a second ball and place it touching the first, pressing a bit to get a solid joining. Continue making pairs of balls until all the dough is used (makes about eighteen pairs).

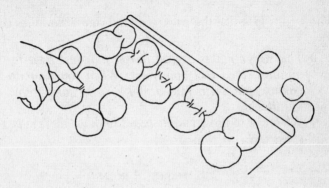

Set to rise in a warm place, covered with a warm, wet towel for about 20 minutes.

Meanwhile, preheat your oven to 375°F.

Bake for about 17 minutes, or until the rolls test done with a toothpick (see page 7).

Cool briefly on a wire rack and serve hot.

Quick-Rising Crescent Rolls

These rolls *look* like the packaged kind, but taste miles better.

◇ *This recipe makes a good freezer roll: Just bake for about 12 minutes, then cool and freeze. When you want to finish the baking, put them into a 400°F. oven for another 10 or 12 minutes.*

◇ *We prefer to use a marble board to shape these rolls; the dough sticks less.*

MAKES 24 ROLLS

2 cups unbleached enriched white flour
1 teaspoon salt
2 packages quick-rising yeast
¼ cup honey
1 cup hot nonfat milk (about 125°F., see page 9)

2 large eggs, at room temperature
¼ cup oil
½ cup wheat germ
2½ to 2¾ cups unbleached enriched white flour (additional)
1 tablespoon caraway seeds.

In a large mixing bowl, combine the 2 cups of flour, the salt, and yeast, and stir well.

Combine the honey and milk.

Stir the milk-and-honey mixture into the flour, and beat for about 5 minutes with a mixer (about 10 minutes by hand), until the batter is quite elastic.

Add the eggs, oil, and wheat germ, and beat for another 2 minutes (about 4 minutes by hand).

Beat in another 2 cups of flour, ½ cup at a time, switching to a wooden spoon when the batter gets stiff.

Sprinkle ¼ cup of flour onto the kneading board, scrape the dough onto it, then sprinkle another ¼ cup over the top, and work in the flour.

Now, knead for about 5 minutes, working in as much of that last ¼ cup as required to make the dough smooth and elastic, but not dry or stiff. (This makes a total of about 4¾ cups of flour.)

Oil a large bowl with a tablespoon of oil, put in the dough and turn to oil all sides. Then set to rise, covered with a dry towel, in a very warm, draft-free place, until the dough has doubled and passes the finger test (page 6)—about 45 minutes.

Grease two baking sheets.

When the dough is risen, punch it down and knead for a little while in the bowl. Then divide it in half.

Flour the kneading board lightly. Shape one half of the dough into a ball, place it on the board, and roll it out into a pizza-like circle about a foot across and no more than ¼ inch thick.

Flour a knife and cut the circle into equal quarters, then cut each quarter into three wedges.

Roll each wedge up from the outside edge, rolling tightly, and pulling the soon-to-be crescent gently to make it a little longer and thinner. Pinch the point into the roll.

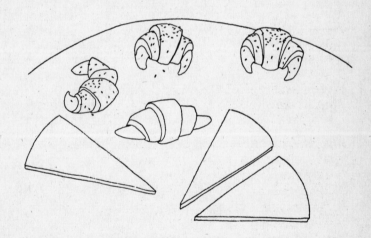

Sprinkle some of the caraway seeds onto a large plate, and roll each piece over some of the seeds.

Place on a greased baking sheet, point down, and curve the ends into a crescent.

Repeat until all the rolls are formed, shaped, seeded, and on the sheets. Leave room for some rise, but fit twelve on each sheet.

Cover the sheets with a dry towel and set in a barely warm place (about 80°F.) to rise for about 20 minutes, until quite puffy.

Starting in a cold oven set at 400°F., bake about 25 minutes, until the tops are golden and the bottoms are a deeper brown. (With our oven, we reverse top and bottom sheets after about 15 minutes.)

Serve directly from the oven.

Rolls

ROLLS have all sorts of advantages over breads. They bake up more quickly (though they make up more slowly), they allow you to vary seeds and flavorings, they invite the participation of very young bakers, and they just seem more festive than bread.

In this chapter we give recipes specifically for rolls, and techniques for shaping rolls. But actually, almost any recipe in this book could be divided into smaller pieces—or spooned into smaller baking containers—and turned into rolls. Be creative.

◊ *Brown-and-Serve Rolls: With the exception of Egg Twist Rolls, all of these rolls can be half-baked, frozen, and then browned and served. Bake about 10 minutes less than the roll recipe, cool on a wire rack, bag or wrap, and put into the freezer. When you want to bake them, preheat your oven to the original temperature, and bake for about an additional 15 minutes— just long enough to brown the outside and heat the inside.*

◊ *For other roll recipes, see the latter part of Chapter 4.*

Egg Twist Rolls

This is a super sandwich roll—just the right size. Egg breads and rolls make the best French toast you can imagine, even straight out of the freezer.

> ◊ We use our marble slab for kneading this bread, as we do for all rich breads (breads with eggs and oil). If you use a wooden board, you will work in more flour—and wind up with a less rich dough.

The Dough:

2 cups unbleached enriched white flour
½ cup wheat germ
2 packages quick-rising yeast
1 teaspoon salt
1¼ cups hot water (125°F., see page 9)

½ cup unsaturated oil
½ cup honey
3 large eggs, at room temperature
3½ to 4 cups unbleached enriched white flour (additional)

The Glaze:

1 egg white

3 tablespoons sesame seeds

Into a large bowl, measure the 2 cups of flour, the wheat germ, yeast, and salt, and stir until fairly uniform.

Add the water, and stir in.

Measure the oil and honey into a saucepan, warm to about 125°F. and add to the bowl. Mix it in with an electric beater, or beat it vigorously by hand with a whisk.

Break the eggs into the bowl and beat them in.

Continue beating for about 5 minutes if by machine (or about 10 minutes by hand), until the batter is quite elastic.

Clean off the beaters or whisk (see page 11) and continue with a wooden spoon.

Add 2½ cups of the additional flour and stir it in thoroughly with a wooden spoon. This should make the batter thick, but not dry enough to knead.

Sprinkle ½ cup of flour onto your kneading board, scrape the batter onto the flour, then sprinkle some more flour on top.

Begin by kneading gently, working in that ½ to 1 cup of remaining flour (total of 5½ to 6 cups of flour). Then dust your hands and continue kneading vigorously—10 to 12 minutes in all. The dough should stop sticking, but not be dry.

Pour a teaspoon or two of oil into the bottom of the scraped-out mixing bowl, put in the dough, and turn it until it is oiled all over.

Cover with a dry towel and set to rise in a warm, draft-free place for about ½ hour, or until the dough is well risen and passes the finger test (see page 6).

Knead the dough gently in the bowl to get rid of the larger bubbles.

Grease the bottoms and sides of two 11 × 16-inch baking sheets.

Scrape the dough onto the kneading board and cut the dough into sixteen roughly equal pieces.

Roll a piece of dough into a rod about a foot long.

Hold a couple of inches of one end of the rod in one hand and form a loop (as if you were making a slip knot). Pass a loop of the dough into the loop you've made (see illustration) and gather the ends of dough onto the bottom of the roll.

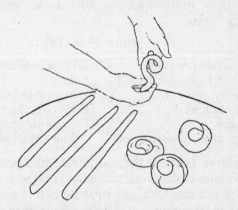

Place the roll on the baking sheet (you will put eight evenly spaced rolls on each sheet), and continue shaping rolls.

When you have all sixteen rolled and placed, cover with a dry towel and set to rise in a warm place for about 15 minutes, or until the rolls are well risen (about 25 percent bigger). Don't worry if they touch, they will break apart after baking.

To glaze the rolls: Beat the egg white for a moment, then gently brush some onto each roll with a pastry brush, covering all the tops. Sprinkle about ½ teaspoon of sesame seeds over the glaze on each roll.

Starting in a cold oven set at 375°F., bake for about 25 minutes, until the tops are browned, and a few rolls pass the doneness test with a toothpick (page 7).

Cool on a wire rack briefly, but serve hot.

Potato Rolls

These are special soft dinner rolls with an individual look (each roll has the shape of a Maltese Cross) and a distinctive flavor. They are much simpler to make than they look.

◊ *There is no salt in this recipe. If you must, add ½ teaspoon.*
◊ *If your mashed potato is cold from the refrigerator, warm it— or at least allow it to come to room temperature. Potato is a wonderful medium for the yeast, so you can expect a lot of rising action.*

MAKES 24 ROLLS

1 package active dry yeast
1¼ cups hot milk (about 125°F., see page 9)
¼ cup unsaturated oil
¼ cup honey
1 large egg, at room temperature

2½ cups unbleached enriched white flour
½ cup cooked well-mashed potato
¼ cup wheat germ
1½ cups unbleached enriched white flour (additional)

In a large bowl, combine the yeast, milk, oil, honey, and egg. Mix.

Add 1½ cups of the flour, stir in, and beat with an electric mixer for about 5 minutes (or about 10 minutes by hand), until elastic.

Beat in the remaining cup of the first flour, then stir in the mashed potato and wheat germ.

Pour about ½ cup of the additional flour onto the kneading board, scrape the batter onto it, then pour a bit more flour over the top.

Knead for about 8 minutes, kneading in the flour on the board and about a cup more (making a total of about 4 cups of flour). The dough should wind up quite smooth, but not dry.

Pour a tablespoon of oil into the bottom of the scraped-out mixing bowl, put the dough in, and turn to oil all sides.

Set to rise, covered with a dry towel, in a very warm, draft-free place until the dough is more than doubled in volume and passes the finger test (page 6)—about 1 hour.

When risen, punch the dough down, sprinkle a little flour onto the board, and cut the dough into four equal pieces.

Lightly grease two large baking sheets.

Cut each piece of dough into thirds. Roll each piece between your palms into a small ball, and place on the baking sheets, twelve per sheet, leaving room for rise and spread.

Now we must snip the rolls to give them their distinctive Maltese-Cross look. With a clean scissors, make four equal snips around the edge of each ball, cutting one quarter of the way through the edge of each ball. This flattens the balls some, of course, but do not worry. The easiest way we've found is to make a snip on one side of all twelve balls, then turn the sheet and snip all twelve on another side, and so on.

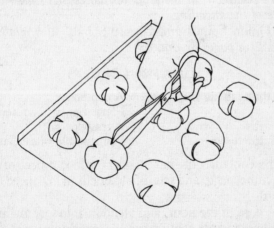

Set to rise, covered with a dry towel, at room temperature (70°F. minimum) for about ½ hour, until well risen.

Preheat your oven to 400°F. and bake for 12 to 14 minutes, until the tops and bottoms are browned, and a couple of rolls pass a doneness test with a toothpick (page 7).

Serve straight from the oven.

Refrigerator Fingers

Here is a terrific technique for those of you who hate to knead but love the fine texture of kneaded bread—or for anyone who wants an easy roll for a dinner party. This dough is prepared about 8 hours in advance with a no-knead blender method and then allowed to rise in the refrigerator until you are ready to cut it into rolls, rise them briefly, and bake.

This batter is mixed in the blender (or food processor)—which makes for very good yeast action. Perhaps this is because the yeast does not clump as it does when you dissolve it in a cup or mixing bowl. At any rate, the end result is incredibly light, even with no kneading.

◊ *Don't skimp on the blending (or processing) time—it takes the place of the kneading.*
◊ *For Onion Spirals and Cheese Spirals, also made with this recipe, see pages 82 and 83.*

MAKES ABOUT 24 ROLLS

1 cup hot milk (about 125°F., see page 9)
1 package active dry yeast
¼ cup unsaturated oil
¼ cup honey
1 large egg, at room temperature
½ teaspoon salt
3 cups whole wheat flour

Put into the container of your blender (or food processor) the milk, yeast, oil, honey, egg, and salt. Blend briefly at low speed (or process at medium).

Add 1¼ cups of the flour, and blend in at low or medium speed. Continue to blend for about a minute, making certain that all the batter circulates through the blades.

Pour and scrape the contents of the blender into a 3-quart bowl, cover with a warm, wet towel, and put in a warm, draft-free place to rise until more than doubled—about 1 hour.

When risen, stir down until it is again its original size. Add ½ cup of flour, and beat in vigorously with a wooden spoon, for a few dozen strokes.

Add another ½ cup of flour and beat again.

Add the remainder of the flour, and beat until all the flour is moistened. Even now, this is so moist it can hardly be called a dough.

Cover with a wet towel and put to rise in your refrigerator for 7 or 8 hours (or overnight). The batter will rise and fall, and then possibly rerise. Left any longer than overnight, the dough will develop a winey flavor.

When ready, remove from the refrigerator. The batter will be much drier, but still somewhat sticky. Flour the board and your hands. Punch down the dough, then scrape it onto the board.

Flour your rolling pin and roll the dough into an even rectangle 6 by 10 inches and about ½ inch thick with square corners (see page 57).

Cut the dough into two 5 by 6-inch halves, and then cut each half into ½-inch-wide strips. (If you want smaller rolls, make two cuts lengthwise, but stick with the ½-inch width.)

Grease a large baking sheet and place the strips of dough on the sheet, leaving about an inch of rising room between each.

Preheat the oven to 400°F.

Cover the sheet with a dry towel and put it in a warm place for about 20 minutes. You should see some rise.

Bake for about 11 minutes, or until the bottoms are browned.

Cool briefly on a wire rack and serve hot.

Onion Spirals

Going to a bring-along party? These can't be beat, and they are easy, as well, because they are made with the no-knead blender method (see Refrigerator Fingers, page 80).

MAKES ABOUT 18 ROLLS

The Dough:

1 recipe Refrigerator Fingers (page 80)

The Filling:

1 pound chopped onions
2 tablespoons unsaturated oil

2 tablespoons poppy seeds

Make the dough for Refrigerator Fingers, up through the refrigerator rise.

Meanwhile, prepare the onion filling: Cook the onions in the oil until they are browned. Mix with the poppy seeds and set aside to cool slightly. (This makes about 1¼ cups of filling.)

When the dough is ready, remove it from the refrigerator, punch it down, sprinkle a little flour on the kneading board, and turn the dough out onto the board. Roll to about ¼-inch thick in a rectangle, about 14 by 10 inches. Turn over a few times, flouring as necessary. Make the corners as square as you can (see page 57).

Spread the filling over most of the rolled-out dough, leaving about 2 inches of one long side bare. Wet that 2-inch strip with water. Begin to roll up tightly from the opposite side. Roll the dough over the watered section—the water will act as a glue to seal off the spiral.

Take a sharp knife, and cut slices from the spiral—rounds about ½ inch wide. You should get about eighteen rounds.

Grease two baking sheets and place nine rounds on each sheet.

Put to rise in a warm place, covered with a dry towel, for about 20 minutes. There will be a good deal of rise.

Starting in a cold oven set for 400°F., bake for about 20 minutes.

Cool briefly on a wire rack, or eat hot from the oven.

Cheese Spirals

These rolls are spicy and delicious—what's more, they are made with the easy no-knead blender method.

MAKES ABOUT 24 ROLLS

The Dough:

1 recipe Refrigerator Fingers (page 80)

The Filling:

1 cup grated sharp cheddar cheese   1 teaspoon fresh-ground black pepper

Prepare the dough for Refrigerator Fingers, up through the refrigerator rise.

Grease two large baking sheets.

Punch down the dough. With a floured rolling pin, roll it out on a floured board until it is about ¼ inch thick. Roll it into a rectangle with corners as square as you can get, (see page 57) about 14 by 10 inches. Turn the dough over as you roll, and dust the board with flour at each turn.

Spread the cheese onto the dough, leaving a bare 2-inch strip down one long side, then sprinkle the pepper over the cheese. With your fingers, wet that bare 2 inches.

Starting from the dry side, roll up the dough into a tight spiral, finishing by rolling over onto the wet dough. The water "glues" the spiral closed.

Cut the spiral in four pieces and each quarter into six round slices, less than ½ inch wide. Place the rounds on the baking sheets, twelve per sheet, leaving enough room to spread.

Cover with a dry towel, and allow to rise at room temperature (70°F. minimum) for about 20 minutes, or until a puffing is visible.

Starting in a cold oven set at 350°F., bake for 20 to 25 minutes, or until the rolls are lightly browned above and golden below.

Cool briefly on a wire rack and serve hot.

"Brown-and-Serve" Crunchy Caraway Squares

The reality of "brown-and-serve" rolls is that almost any roll can be partially baked—until the yeast is killed (so there is no further swelling) and the outside hard enough to handle—frozen, and then browned and served when wanted.

The advantage of these squares is that they are shaped for easy handling and thorough reheating—as well as being deliciously crunchy.

2½ cups whole wheat flour
1 teaspoon salt
1 tablespoon caraway seed
1 package active dry yeast
1½ cups warm nonfat milk (about 110°F., see page 9)
2 tablespoons unsaturated oil

2 tablespoons honey
½ cup yellow cornmeal
1½ cups whole wheat flour (additional)
2 tablespoons yellow cornmeal (additional)

In a large bowl, combine the 2½ cups of whole wheat flour with the salt and caraway seeds.

Dissolve the yeast in warm (not hot) milk, stir in the oil and honey. Stir this mixture into the flour.

Beat for about 5 minutes with an electric mixer (or about 10 minutes by hand with a whisk), until some elasticity is developed.

Switch to a wooden spoon and beat in the ½ cup of cornmeal, then ½ cup of flour.

Spread ¼ cup of flour on the kneading board, scrape the dough onto it, sprinkle another ¼ cup of flour on top, and work it in.

Knead for a total of 10 minutes, or until the dough is medium-dry and quite responsive, adding as much of the final ½ cup of flour as necessary. Dust the board and your hands with additional whole wheat flour as you need. (You will have used about 4 cups of flour in all.)

Pour a teaspoon of oil into the scraped-out mixing bowl, put in the dough, and turn it to oil all sides.

Set to rise, covered with a warm, wet towel, in a warm, draft-free place for about 1 hour, or until about doubled in volume and the dough passes a finger test (page 6).

Grease a large baking sheet, and sprinkle it with the additional cornmeal.

When risen, punch the dough down in the bowl, and sprinkle a little flour onto your kneading board and rolling pin. Roll the dough out to a large rectangle, about 12 by 16 inches and about ⅛ inch thick. Make the corners as square as you can (see page 57).

Cut the rectangle into twenty-four squares (about 2½ inches each) and place on the baking sheet, leaving about 1 inch between pieces.

Rise at room temperature (70°F. minimum), covered with a dry towel, for about 45 minutes, or until the squares have puffed a little.

If making "Brown-and-Serve": Starting in a cold oven set at 375°F., bake for about 15 minutes—until rising stops and the bottoms just begin to color.

At this stage (they are not done, remember), remove from the oven, cool thoroughly on a wire rack, then seal into a plastic bag and freeze.

To reheat the frozen rolls, set the oven for 400°F., remove the squares from the freezer, and bake on a wire rack (or on the oven rack itself) until the bottoms are golden brown—about 15 to 20 minutes.

If using right away: Start in a cold oven set at 375°F. Bake for 20 to 25 minutes, until the bottoms are golden brown and the rolls test done (page 7).

Rich Whole Wheat Rolls

Rich Whole Wheat Bread dough (see page 24) is a natural for rolls, because the ingredients that make it rich also make it easy to handle. Because they are smaller than bread, rolls tend to get stale more quickly, but these keep very well because they are rich.

MAKES 24 ROLLS

The Dough:

1 recipe Rich Whole Wheat Bread
  (page 24)

The Glaze:

1 egg yolk   2 tablespoons poppy seeds
1 tablespoon water

Prepare the recipe for Rich Whole Wheat Bread, rise it, punch it down, and knead briefly to make a cohesive mass.

Grease two large baking sheets.

Pinch off lumps of dough and form into flat circles 3 inches in diameter and about 1 inch thick. Place the rounds of dough onto the baking sheets, twelve to a sheet, leaving an inch or more space between each.

Take a knife with a smooth, undecorated metal handle and press the handle lengthwise firmly and evenly all the way across each

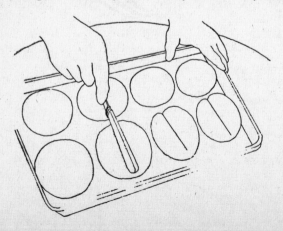

roll, almost down to the sheet. This divides the roll about in half. Do not fold it. (If the knife handle sticks, wiggle the knife to free it, and dust the handle lightly with flour.)

Cover with a dry towel and set to rise for ½ hour in a very warm, draft-free place.

To glaze the rolls: Mix the egg yolk with the water and beat until smooth. Brush the yolk over the surfaces gently with a pastry brush and sprinkle with poppy seeds.

Starting in a cold oven set at 375°F., bake for about 20 minutes, or until the tops have turned a golden brown and the bottoms have darkened.

Cool briefly on a wire rack and serve hot.

Kaiser Rolls

On his birthday, the German Kaiser distributed white rolls of this sort to his subjects. (They ate brown bread the rest of the year.)

These rolls can be made from many of the doughs in this book. French Bread works very well, as does 100% Whole Wheat. We usually use Spiral Bread dough, making sure we substitute wheat germ and bran for part of the white flour. The technique is the same whatever dough you use.

◇ *These rolls start out as a disk of dough, but end up in a pinwheel shape. The center of the "pinwheel" must be pressed firmly to make sure the roll does not open in the baking.*

◇ *To develop the crust, we spray the rolls with water and put a pan of water in the bottom of the oven during baking to raise the humidity. For a softer roll, you can omit the spraying and glazing, and reduce the baking time to about 20 minutes.*

◇ *The glaze is not put on until the rolls have baked for 15 minutes.*

◇ *If you do not wish to make twenty-four rolls, divide the dough in thirds, store two of the thirds in the refrigerator or freezer (see page 232), and shape only eight kaisers.*

MAKES 24 ROLLS

The Dough:

1 recipe Spiral Bread (see page 47)

The Glaze:

1 egg white	2 to 3 tablespoons seeds (poppy,
1 teaspoon water	sesame, caraway, or Russian car-
	away)

Prepare the recipe for Spiral Bread, rise it, punch it down, and knead it briefly into a cohesive mass.

Grease three large baking sheets.

Pinch off 2-inch balls of dough and roll them between your palms until round. You will wind up with 24 balls.

Flour your board lightly, and flatten a ball into a disk 4½ to 5 inches across.

Take one edge of the circle, pull it gently to make a small point, and lift that point over into the center of the disk. Press it into the center, then press all along the right side of the triangle you've just made (A).

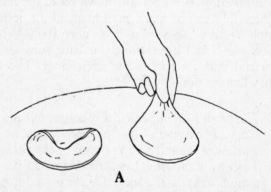

A

Move to the right and lift the point which you've just created by pressing the seam; bring this point into the center of the disk, slightly overlapping the first fold (B). Once more, press with your finger along the right side edge.

Again, move to the right, lift the point your pressing has created, press it into the center, and press the right side edge (C).

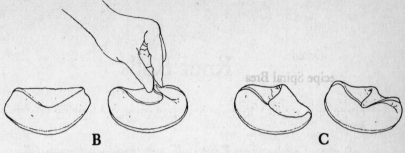

B   C

Repeat this process four more times (seven lifts in all)—but on the last lift, you press down firmly into the center and do not seal any edge (D).

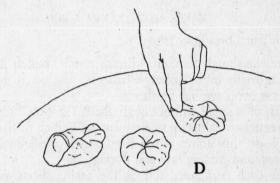

D

Place each roll on a greased baking sheet as finished, leaving about 1 inch between rolls for rise—eight rolls per sheet.

Cover the rolls with a dry towel, and set to rise in a warm place for about ½ hour.

Just before baking, boil 2 cups of water. Put a cake pan into the bottom of the oven and pour in the water.

When the rolls are risen, spray with tepid water.

Starting in a cold oven set for 350°F., bake for 25 to 30 minutes.

After 5 minutes of baking, pull the trays forward and spray the rolls again.

To glaze the rolls: Beat the egg white and water together and, after 15 minutes of baking, pull the rolls forward, brush the egg white onto the surfaces gently with a pastry brush, and quickly sprinkle on the seeds, about ¼ teaspoon of seeds per roll.

When the rolls test done (see page 7), remove and cool briefly on a wire rack. Serve warm.

Knot Rolls

These rolls are easy to make and they come out looking very professional.

◊ *If you wish a Tan Knot Roll, substitute whole wheat flour for up to half of the white flour.*

◊ *If you do not wish to make forty-eight rolls, freeze or refrigerate half or three quarters of the dough.*

MAKES ABOUT 48 SMALL ROLLS

1 recipe Spiral Bread (see page 47)

Prepare the dough for Spiral Bread, rise it, punch it down, and knead it briefly into a cohesive ball.

Grease two large baking sheets.

Pinch off a small ball of dough about 1½ inch through and roll it between your palms into a strand about ½ inch thick and 8 inches long. Twist this strand into a simple overhand knot by making a little loop and passing one end through it.

Place each completed roll on the baking sheets as you finish, about twenty-four to a sheet.

Cover with a dry towel and rise for about ½ hour in a warm, draft-free place.

Starting in a cold oven set at 350°F., bake for about 20 minutes, or until a couple of the knots test done with a toothpick (see page 7).

Serve hot.

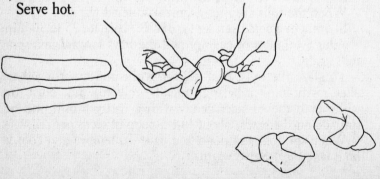

∽⌾ 6 ⌾∽

Ethnic Plain Breads

IT'S nice to have friends from exotic places. These breads are reminders of our exotic friends. And they are easy to make.

TORTILLAS

Tortillas are Mexican flat cakes, cooked on an unoiled hot griddle, and made without yeast—so they do not rise. A meal does not have to be Mexican to welcome tortillas as an accompaniment.

Tortillas are fun to eat, but they are best hot off the griddle, which means the tortilla-chef stands and cooks while everyone else enjoys hot tortillas with his meal.

◊ *Your griddle should be large enough to cook two tortillas at a time.*
◊ *Tortillas should be served hot and flexible. We give the timing on our griddle, but you may have to experiment with your own. At any rate, don't overcook them: They should not be stiff.*
◊ *Because they are more cohesive, whole wheat flour tortillas can be formed and stored overnight, for cooking mañana. Don't try this with the more fragile corn flour and cornmeal tortillas.*

Corn-Flour Tortillas

We make traditional corn-flour tortillas with Masa Harina, a trademark of the Quaker Company. Quaker soaks the corn in limestone and water. This softens the kernel and gives it a distinctive flavor. Then the whole grain is ground into a flour. Their package gives a recipe for tortillas, but we find our own recipe a little easier to handle.

◊ *Tortillas are strictly a "with meals" bread, so don't put them on the griddle until the rest of the meal is about ready.*

MAKES 8 TORTILLAS*

1 cup Masa Harina   1 tablespoon unsaturated oil
½ cup warm water (100° to 110°F.,
    see page 9)

Preheat your griddle to very high heat.

Mix together the flour, water, and oil to make a cohesive mass. If your mass is a crumbly mess, add another tablespoon of oil or water. You must be able to shape this mixture into a ball.

Divide into eight equal pieces and roll each piece between your palms to make a ball.

To shape into the traditional flat pancakes, take a food-storage size plastic bag (we buy one called "gallon-size," which measures 9½ by 13½ inches flat), place it on a firm surface, put one of the balls on the bag, and fold the bag in half over the ball. With the heel of your hand or with a rolling pin, flatten to a very thin pancake about 5 inches across.

Lift the bag off the top of the pancake, place the pancake on your palm, then peel off the other half of the bag; place the pancake on your hot griddle.

Cook for about 1 minute on the first side, then turn and cook for another 1 to 2 minutes on the other. The tortilla should be touched with brown, but not dark.

Serve as they come off the griddle.

---

* This recipe is easily doubled for sixteen tortillas.

Whole-Wheat-Flour Tortillas

This corn-free tortilla is very popular with some devotees of Tex-Mex cooking.

◊ *We have had no trouble rolling these all out the day before, placing baker's parchment or waxed paper between the pancakes, and storing them, raw, in the refrigerator overnight for next-day cooking.*

MAKES 8 TORTILLAS

1 cup plus 1 tablespoon whole wheat flour
¼ teaspoon salt

¼ cup water
2 tablespoons unsaturated oil

Preheat your griddle to very hot.

Combine all the ingredients, and mix well with a fork until the mixture can be shaped into a large, cohesive ball.

Divide into eight pieces and shape and cook as you did with Corn-Flour Tortillas, on page 92.

Cornmeal Tortillas

If you cannot find Masa Harina—or you do not cook tortillas often enough to make it worthwhile to buy it—you can make tortillas with cornmeal.

MAKES 12 TORTILLAS

1 cup plus 1 tablespoon yellow cornmeal
¼ teaspoon salt

1 cup water
1 tablespoon unsaturated oil

Preheat your griddle to very hot.

Measure the cornmeal and salt into a mixing bowl.

Combine the water and oil, bring to a boil and pour over the cornmeal. Stir well until the mixture can be formed into a cohesive ball.

Divide the mixture into twelve parts, roll or press out to make 4- to 5-inch pancakes, following the directions for Corn-Flour Tortillas on page 92.

These tortillas are somewhat fragile, and if they don't get to the griddle quite flat, flatten them a little with your pancake turner.

Cook as directed for Corn-Flour Tortillas, page 92.

Corn Dodger

The late singer Lee Hayes collected a folk song that told of a mean Arkansas employer who charged him half a dollar (a day's pay then) for a meal of unchewable meat and corn dodger.

The corn dodger is "poverty" bread. However, when baked until crisp on top and bottom and tender in the middle, it is delicious with stews or gravies.

MAKES 1 8-INCH-SQUARE PAN

2¼ cups water
½ teaspoon salt

1 tablespoon unsaturated oil
2 cups yellow cornmeal

Preheat your oven to 400°F.

Bring the water, salt, and oil to a boil.

Measure the cornmeal into a large bowl, and pour the boiling water over it, stirring briskly with a fork until all the water is absorbed.

Grease an 8-inch square pan, and spread the mixture over the bottom in an even ½-inch layer.

Bake for about 45 minutes, until the top is crisp, but not browned.

Cut into squares and serve hot.

Chappatis

This East Indian favorite is the simplest bread you can make: no yeast, no rising, not even an oven. It is a flatbread cooked on a griddle or in a heavy frying pan, without any oil.

◊ *If your taste demands it, add ¼ teaspoon of salt to the dough, but do try it without first.*

◊ *If you only wish to serve a few chappatis, roll out the extras, place them individually on sheets of waxed paper or baker's parchment, wrap, and freeze. When you are ready to have them, just unwrap and cook as below.*

◊ *Leftover cooked chappatis make good crackers if allowed to dry before storing.*

MAKES 8 CHAPPATIS

2 cups whole wheat flour   ¾ cup water

Into a large bowl, measure 1 cup of the flour and all the water. Beat with an electric mixer, at medium speed, for about 5 minutes, or until the batter becomes quite elastic. (You can also mix this by hand with a whisk, but it will require twice as much beating.)

Clean the beaters into the bowl (see page 11), mix in about half the remaining flour, and stir in well. The dough should now have the consistency of well-cooked oatmeal.

Put half of the remaining flour on the kneading board, scrape out the dough onto it, dust the top, and knead for about 7 minutes, sprinkling the dough lightly with the remaining flour as required. Do not force the flour in. (If you prefer, you can knead this right in the bowl.) You should wind up with a medium-stiff dough.

When kneaded, shape the dough into a ball, cut in half, cut each half in half, and then in half again, winding up with eight pieces. Roll each piece into a ball and set on a plate to rest for about 20 minutes.

Preheat your griddle or a heavy skillet without oil until it is very hot.

Sprinkle a small bit of flour on the board and on your rolling pin, and roll one ball into a very thin circle, about 6 inches across.

One at a time, place the chappati on the griddle and cook about 2½ minutes per side. With a spatula, press down any bumps that come up. While one cooks, roll out the next.

Serve with the meal as they come off the griddle, or keep warm and serve several at a time.

Nan

This East Indian bread is worked with a dough that is barely dry enough to handle. Because it is so sticky, it should not be a beginner's first kneaded bread.

Nan looks much like oval pitas but has a richer taste.

Sesame oil gives nan a nice Oriental flavor.

◊ *When kneading, use only the fronts of your fingers—don't dig in or press hard, as you would with most doughs. And knead with only one hand. Keep the other hand clean and dry to get you unstuck, and to add more flour as you knead.*

MAKES 12 OVALS

The Dough:

1 package active dry yeast	1 large egg, at room temperature
1 tablespoon honey	1 cup hot water (about 125°F., see
1 teaspoon salt	page 9)
¼ cup sesame oil	3¼ to 4 cups unbleached enriched
¼ cup yogurt or buttermilk	white flour

The Glaze:

melted butter	poppy seeds

Preheat your oven to 450°F.

Into a large mixing bowl, measure the yeast, honey, salt, oil, and yogurt. Stir together.

Mix in the egg, add the hot water, and stir.

Mix in the first 3 cups of flour, 1 cup at a time, mixing each cupful well with a wooden spoon.

Flour your hand, and add more flour to the bowl a little at a time, kneading with the fronts of the fingers of one hand, until the dough shows the first signs of not sticking.

From time to time, clean your hand off with a spoon (and then reflour), because dough tends to stick to dough.

Somewhere past 3¼ cups of flour, you should be just able to handle the dough—gingerly.

Scrape the dough down off the sides of the bowl, onto the ball at the bottom. Cover with a dry towel and set to rise in a warm, draft-free place for about 1 hour. Finger test for rise (see page 6).

When risen, flour your hand again, punch the dough down, and knead briefly to get rid of the larger bubbles.

Flour the kneading board. Scrape the dough ball out onto the board, and cut into twelve roughly equal pieces.

With floured hands, roll each piece into a ball and place on the board to rise for 10 minutes, covered with a dry towel.

Grease a large baking sheet—once for the whole batch.

Flour your hands lightly and pick up the first ball. Flatten it between your hands to an oval no more than ¼ inch thick.

Lay the oval on the baking sheet, leaving room for another, and press it a little flatter with the flat of your hand.

Repeat with a second ball.

To glaze the bread: Dip a pastry brush into the melted butter and brush the tops of the flat loaves, then sprinkle with a pinch or two of poppy seeds.

Bake by placing the sheet directly on the bottom of the oven—not on a rack, but on the metal divider directly over the flame or heating element (see page 102).

Bake about 5 minutes, or until the bottom color is dark brown. If the tops are too pale, slip the sheet under the broiler for 20 to 30 seconds.

Serve as soon as they come from the oven. You'll seldom get bigger compliments.

PIZZA

Pizza as we know it in the States isn't *the* pizza but *a* pizza, because in Italian *pizza* means anything that is flat and round and baked like a pie. In Ventimiglia, we ate "pizza" that was like toasted Wonder Bread, with the thinnest smearing of tomato sauce and an eighth of a black olive in the middle of each rectangular slice!

The crust for our pizza is thinner than you'll find in most pizzerias. And the toppings we make never see canned tomato sauce.

◊ *We don't use a specific pizza dough; instead, we use Rich Whole Wheat Bread dough—or whatever plain yeast-bread dough we feel like. (French Bread dough also works well.) We bake up half the risen and punched down dough as bread or rolls and save the other half for pizza—or vice versa.*

◊ *Half of any yeast-bread recipe in this book using 6 or more cups of flour should yield two pizzas.*

◊ *If we use a white dough, we always enrich it with wheat germ and bran.*

◊ *Get out your utensils—two cookie sheets and a rolling pin— before you begin; your hands will soon get oily.*

The Dough:

½ recipe for Rich Whole Wheat
Bread (page 24)

3 tablespoons olive oil

The Topping:

Topping of your choice (see below)
2 tablespoons grated Parmesan
cheese (and/or)

¼ cup grated mozzarella cheese

Preheat your oven to 450°F.

Assuming that you have been keeping the dough in the refrigerator, remove it, uncover the bowl, pour the olive oil over the top, and knead for about 30 seconds.

Cut the dough in half, in the bowl.

Take one well-oiled half from the bowl and place it on an unfloured kneading board. With stiff fingers, poke it flat into a rectangle or circle.

Now, with a rolling pin, roll the dough flat and very thin (about ⅛ inch) into a circle or rectangle to fit your cookie sheet.

Carefully transfer the dough to an ungreased sheet, folding up the rim of the dough slightly to create a raised edge.

Repeat for the second pizza.

If there is any oil left in the bowl, brush or smear it over the top of the dough.

Bake for about 15 minutes, or until the dough shell is crisp.

In the meantime, prepare the topping.

Toppings

Here are two of our favorite toppings. Vary or even combine these according to your taste, or create your own.

Zucchini Topping

COVERS 2 PIZZAS

3 tablespoons olive oil
1 large onion (chopped)
2 cloves garlic (minced)
2 to 2½ pounds zucchini (washed, trimmed)

1 tablespoon dried oregano
2 tablespoons dried basil
1 teaspoon fennel seed
½ teaspoon salt

Pour the oil into a large skillet and add the onion and garlic. Cover and cook over a medium flame.

Cut the unpeeled zucchini into ¼-inch slices, and, when the onions and garlic are browned, add to the skillet, along with the remaining ingredients, and stir.

Cover and cook over a medium flame for about 20 minutes, stirring occasionally.

Quick Tomato Topping

◊ *These don't have to be hothouse tomatoes—the cheapest are as tasty as the best, after cooking. Just make sure they are ripe. They can even be overripe.*

COVERS 2 PIZZAS

2 tablespoons olive oil
10 large juicy tomatoes (washed, chopped, unpeeled)
1 tablespoon dried basil

2 teaspoons fennel seed
¼ teaspoon salt
garlic powder

Pour the oil into a large skillet and add the tomatoes, basil, fennel, and salt. Stir and sprinkle with garlic powder to taste.

Cover and cook over a high flame for only about 6 minutes. Lift the cover only to mash the tomatoes into a mush after 4 or 5 minutes.

When topping the pizza, spoon out with a slotted spoon, leaving as much of the watery liquid in the skillet as possible.

Adding the Topping

Remove the pizza shells from the oven and immediately spoon the cooked topping (still hot) over them, being careful not to cover the raised rim. Sprinkle each with half the grated Parmesan and mozzarella cheese.

Return the pizzas to the hot oven and bake for another few minutes, just long enough to melt the cheese.

Serve hot. A pizza wheel cuts this best, but a carefully wielded knife will do.

Pita

The word *pita* is Greek for pie. But you don't have to be Middle Eastern to make and enjoy pita.

Our pita is a round flat bread, about 5 inches across that forms an internal pouch in the baking. It is great plain, hot from the oven, or split and filled with almost anything. It even makes great hamburger rolls. In Middle Eastern restaurants it is sometimes served cut in wedges for dipping into tahini.

◇ *The dough is first formed into balls, then flattened into smooth rounds about ¼ inch thick. Creases or pinches left in the rounds inhibit the rising, and you lose your chance for a pouch along a pinch. If you have patched the dough or you see a crease, roll that ball between your hands until the crease goes away.*

◇ *Greek and Armenian bakers of the older generation bake pita directly on the bottom of the oven—on that metal divider directly over the flame or heating element. They will flip the flattened rounds onto that bottom divider and then pull them out with a long-handled spatula or a baker's peel (see page 234). We do almost the same thing but we use a baking sheet large enough to hold two pitas at a time, and put the sheet onto that metal divider.*

◇ *Bottom color is the doneness-indicator for this bread. It has the tendency to go dark on the bottom and to be completely baked, while the top is still pale. If the bottom shows dark but the top is light, put the baking sheet under the broiler for 20 to 30 seconds to brown on top.*

Traditional Pita

MAKES 12 PITAS

1 package active dry yeast
2 tablespoons honey
1 teaspoon salt
2 cups hot water (about 125°F., see
  page 9)

5 to 6 cups unbleached enriched
  white flour

In a large bowl, combine the yeast, honey, salt, and hot water, and stir well.

Add the first 4 cups of flour, 1 cup at a time, mixing each cup in well with a wooden spoon.

Spread 1 cup of flour over the kneading board, scrape the dough onto it, and knead in.

Add as much of the remaining cup of flour as required to make a medium-stiff dough, then knead for a few more minutes.

Drip a teaspoon of oil into the scraped-out mixing bowl, put the dough ball into the bowl, and turn it to oil all sides.

Cover with a dry towel and set to rise in a very warm, draft-free place for about 1 hour.

When the finger test (see page 6) shows the dough has risen, punch it down and knead it gently in the bowl for a moment to get rid of any big bubbles.

Preheat your oven to 450°F.

Turn the risen dough onto a lightly floured board, and cut it into twelve roughly equal pieces.

Roll each piece into a ball (you may need to flour your hands lightly), and place each ball onto the floured board. Cover with a dry towel and let rest for 10 minutes.

Grease a large baking sheet.

Now, because the balls have rested, the tops have dried slightly. Lay the dry side on the board and, with the palm of your hand, pat, press, and pound (but don't poke) until the ball is flattened into a round of dough about ¼ inch thick and 5 inches across.

Gently lift this round of dough from the board and lay it on the greased sheet, leaving room for another. Flatten it a bit more on the sheet.

Repeat for the second ball.

Put the baking sheet directly on the bottom of the oven and bake for about 5 minutes, or until the bottom color shows dark brown.

Serve straight from the oven and flatten your next pair and bake similarly.

Repeat with the remaining pitas. (Do not regrease the baking sheet.)

If wanted for sandwiches, cool briefly on a wire rack, then slit one side and insert the filling.

Whole Wheat Quick-Rising Mini-Pita

Whole wheat flour makes just as good a pocket—and an even better flavor.

◊ *If you prefer, shape into twelve large pitas instead of the twenty-four miniatures called for.*

◊ *As with traditional pita, do not pinch the dough or leave wrinkles in it. That keeps the pouch from forming.*

MAKES 24 MINIATURE PITAS

3 cups whole wheat flour
1 package quick-rising yeast
1 teaspoon salt
2 cups hot water (about 125°F., see page 9)

2 to 3 cups whole wheat flour (additional)

In a large bowl, combine the first flour, yeast, and salt. Stir.

Add the water and stir well.

Beat with an electric mixer for about 3 minutes (or about 6 minutes by hand).

With a wooden spoon, beat in 1½ cups of the additional flour, ½ cup at a time.

Dump ½ cup of flour onto the kneading board, scrape the batter out onto it, turn it over, and begin to work in the flour.

Knead in as much of an additional ½ cup of flour as required to make a cohesive, but not dry, dough. Knead briskly for another 3 minutes, dusting your hands with flour as necessary.

When the dough is kneaded, drip a tablespoon of oil into the bowl, put in the dough, and turn it to oil all sides.

Set to rise, covered with a warm, wet towel in a very warm, draft-free place, for about ½ hour, or until the dough passes the finger test (see page 6).

Preheat your oven to 450°F.

Grease two large baking sheets.

With a lightly floured hand, punch down the dough and knead easily for a minute or less to get rid of the larger bubbles.

Dust the kneading board with flour.

Divide the dough into twenty-four pieces, roll each piece into a smooth ball, place each ball on the floured board, and allow to rest for about 5 minutes.

Turn a ball over, flatten it to ¼ inch or a little less (the diameter will be 3½ to 4 inches), place it on a baking sheet, and repeat until you have nine minis on the sheet.

Pat down the pitas just before they go in the oven.

Place the sheet directly on the bottom of the oven, on the metal divider over the flame or heating element, and bake for about 5 minutes, until the bottoms are brown.

To brown the tops, remove from the oven and place the sheet under the broiler for 30 to 40 seconds.

When the first set is almost baked, prepare the second set and bake similarly.

Repeat with the remaining pitas. (Do not regrease the baking sheet.)

Serve as you would Traditional Pita.

7

Ethnic and Holiday Fancy Breads

HOLIDAY and traditional breads from various ethnic backgrounds are fun. Work, but fun.

Do not let yourself be put off by the long lists of ingredients or the special treatments many of them require. These are special-occasion breads your family and friends will long remember.

IRISH SODA BREAD

This is a darlin' bread, a darlin' bread (if we may borrow from Sean O'Casey). It is equally valuable as a tea bread or a sandwich bread. And it is unique: a soda bread that requires a small amount of kneading.

We provide two versions of Irish soda bread—a traditional version and a "healthier" one. The second recipe substitutes oil for butter and adds some bran—but it comes out much the same.

◊ *Don't skimp on the caraway seeds. When we taste-tested this recipe with less caraway, all three testers independently found the recipe with less caraway less sweet and less flavorful.*

◊ *This bread is baked in a 2-quart casserole (ours is 7½ by 3 inches). The casserole makes for a very crusty crust.*

Basic Irish Soda Bread

MAKES 1 LARGE BREAD IN A 2-QUART CASSEROLE

3¾ cups unbleached enriched white flour
¼ cup wheat germ
½ teaspoon salt
1 teaspoon baking soda
1 teaspoon baking powder
2 tablespoons caraway seeds
¼ cup unsalted butter
1½ cups unsulfured raisins
1⅛ cups yogurt
⅜ cup honey
1 large egg, lightly beaten
3 to 4 tablespoons unbleached enriched white flour (additional)

Preheat your oven to 350°F.

In a large bowl, combine the 3¾ cups of flour and the wheat germ, salt, baking soda, baking powder, and seeds, and mix until uniform.

Blend in the butter with a pastry knife (or rub in with your fingers). Stir in the raisins.

Combine the yogurt, honey, and egg, and mix well. Stir into the dry ingredients until all are moistened, and then continue to stir for another minute or so.

Sprinkle a couple of tablespoons of flour onto the kneading board, scrape the batter onto it, then sprinkle another tablespoon or so over the batter.

Work the batter into a cohesive lump, then knead gently for only a few minutes. Shape the dough into a smooth ball.

Grease a 2-quart casserole, place the dough ball into the casserole, and, with a sharp knife, slash a cross into its top, about ½-inch deep and all the way across.

Bake for 80 to 90 minutes until the top is golden brown and the loaf tests done with a thin knife (see page 7).

Cool on a wire rack and serve warm.

Higher-Fiber Irish Soda Bread

MAKES 1 LARGE BREAD IN A 2-QUART CASSEROLE

3½ cups white unbleached enriched flour
¼ cup wheat germ
¼ cup bran
½ teaspoon salt
1 teaspoon baking soda
1 teaspoon baking powder
2 tablespoons caraway seeds

1½ cups unsulfured raisins
¼ cup unsaturated oil
1 cup yogurt
⅜ cup honey
1 large egg, lightly beaten
3 to 4 tablespoons unbleached enriched white flour (additional)

Preheat your oven to 350°F.

Combine all the dry ingredients in a large bowl, and mix well.

Combine all the wet ingredients in a 2-cup measure, and stir well.

Stir the wet ingredients into the dry until all are moistened, and proceed as for Basic Irish Soda Bread, page 108.

Italian Christmas Bread (Panettone)

The only difficult thing about making this marvelously yeasty Italian fruit bread is finding the proper mold.

Panettone is traditionally baked in slant-sided, undecorated molds (of almost any size). If you cannot find plain molds, use two bundt molds (see page 114) or four Turk's head molds (see page 239)—or any molds with a center post.

◊ *Traditionally, candied fruit (usually citron) is used. We have used dried fruit instead (mango, papaya, apricots, or pineapple), along with raisins or currants and nuts.*
◊ *The glaze is optional, but it helps keep the outside of the bread moist, adds a bit of zing to the flavor, and gives a shiny look.*
◊ *Panettone freezes and then toasts beautifully.*

MAKES 2 LARGE OR 4 SMALL BREADS

The Dough:

2 packages active dry yeast
¾ cup warm water (about 110°F., see page 9)
¾ cup honey, at room temperature
2 cups unbleached enriched white flour
½ teaspoon salt
grated zest of 1 lemon
¾ cup unsaturated oil, at room temperature
3 large eggs, at room temperature

2 tablespoons lemon juice (juice of 1 lemon)
½ cup wheat germ
1 cup unsulfured seedless raisins (or currants)
¼ cup chopped dried mango (or other dried fruit)
1 cup chopped filberts
5 cups unbleached enriched white flour (additional)

The Glaze (optional):

2 tablespoons orange juice

2 tablespoons honey

Dissolve the yeast in the warm water, then stir in the honey. Allow to stand for several minutes, until yeast action begins (a small amount of foam will form on the surface).

In a large bowl, stir together the 2 cups of flour, the salt, and the zest. Pour the yeast mixture over this, stir to wet the flour, and then beat for about 5 minutes with an electric mixer, or 10 minutes by hand, until quite elastic.

Beat in the oil, the eggs, and the lemon juice, until smooth.

Beat in the wheat germ, then the dried fruits and nuts.

Beat in 4 cups of the additional flour, ½ cup at a time, switching over to a wooden spoon when the batter becomes too stiff for the electric beater (or your whisk).

Sprinkle ¼ cup of flour onto the kneading board, scrape the dough onto it, then spread another ¼ cup over the top and begin to knead gently.

Knead for a total of about 8 minutes, working in as much of the last ½ cup of flour as required to get a very elastic and smooth—but not stiff—dough. (This brings you to a total of about 7 cups of flour.)

Pour 1 tablespoon of oil into the scraped-out mixing bowl and put in the dough, turning it to oil all sides. Set to rise, covered with a dry towel, in a very warm, draft-free place until clearly doubled in volume, 1½ hours or more.

When risen, punch the dough down, and knead it gently in the bowl to get rid of the larger bubbles.

Grease two large or four small molds quite well.

Divide the dough in half (or in quarters, if you are using small molds), roll each piece gently into a thick sausage shape, and fit it into a mold, around the center post. The dough should fill the mold less than halfway up.

Put to rise again, covered with a dry towel, for about an hour, or until doubled.

Starting in a cold oven set for 375°F., bake small molds for about 30 minutes, large molds for about 40 minutes. Do not overcook or the panettone will stick to the pan. Test for doneness with a thin knife (see page 7).

Turn out of the molds, and put on a wire rack over a large plate. Glaze immediately.

To glaze: Mix together the orange juice and honey, and brush over the surface with a pastry brush.

Swedish Saffron Wreath

This bread is a beautiful deep yellow inside and a more traditional deep brown outside. The saffron is not just a coloring agent; it is a delicious and delicate spice—as you will discover.

◊ *Saffron is the stigmas of autumn crocus, and it is expensive. Our last purchase—a fraction of a gram—cost almost $5, which comes out to $184 an ounce.*

◊ To powder the saffron, *place the strands on a clean piece of aluminum foil and roll it heavily with a rolling pin; then pile it together and roll again. You will need about thirty of the tiny strands to make the ¼ teaspoon called for.*

MAKES 1 LARGE WREATH

The Dough:

1 cup warm milk (about 110°F. see page 9)
½ cup honey
2 packages active dry yeast
¼ teaspoon powdered saffron (about ¼ gram)
2 cups unbleached enriched white flour

1 large egg, at room temperature
¼ cup unsaturated oil
¼ cup wheat germ
2 tablespoons ground almonds
½ cup unsulfured raisins
2 cups unbleached enriched white flour (additional)

The Glaze:

1 large egg
1 tablespoon water

3 tablespoons ground almonds

Stir together the milk and honey, add the yeast and stir, then stir in the saffron. Allow to stand for a few minutes, until the beginning of yeast activity can be seen.

Put the 2 cups of flour into a large bowl, pour the yeast mixture over it, stir, and then beat for about 5 minutes with an electric mixer, or about 10 minutes by hand.

Beat the egg, then the oil, then the wheat germ in well.

Beat the almonds and raisins in well.

Switch over to a wooden spoon, and beat in 1½ cups of additional flour, ½ cup at a time.

Sprinkle a couple of tablespoons of flour on your kneading board, scrape the dough onto it, then sprinkle a couple of tablespoons more over the dough.

Knead for 6 to 7 minutes, adding as little of the remaining flour as required to make an elastic and smooth dough (bringing the total to about 4 cups of flour). To avoid adding too much flour, for the last few minutes of kneading, sprinkle the flour on your hands, not the dough.

Pour 1 tablespoon of oil into the scraped-out mixing bowl and add the dough, turning it to oil all sides. Then set to rise, covered with a dry towel, in a quite-warm, draft-free place, until the dough is doubled in volume and passes a finger test (see page 6)—1½ to 2 hours.

Grease a large baking sheet.

When risen, punch the dough down and knead briefly and gently in the bowl.

Cut into three equal pieces and roll each piece into a long rope, about 2 inches long. Place side by side and braid the three ropes into an even, long braid (see illustration). Do not pinch the ends. Lift carefuly onto the greased sheet. Join and press the ends into a circle so that you wind up with a wreath.

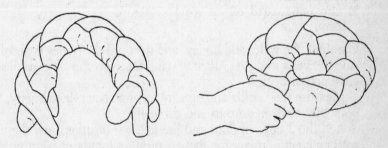

Set to rise, covered with a dry towel, in some gentle warmth or at room temperature (about 70°F.) for about 45 minutes, until it is well risen.

Meanwhile, preheat your oven to 400°F.

Bake for about 20 minutes, or until a toothpick inserted into one of the joints comes out clean.

Cool on a wire rack and serve warm.

Bundt Kuchen

This is a German coffee cake with a delicious crunchy covering of finely chopped nuts.

Bundt pans, unlike some shaped molds, are simple to find. We bought ours in a supermarket, and had a choice of plain or nonstick.

◇ *Vanilla extract (real vanilla, not vanillin) must be fresh to be at its best. If yours is weak or old, use an extra teaspoonful.*

YIELDS 1 LOAF

¼ cup hot water (about 125°F., see page 9)
¾ cup honey, at room temperature
2 packages active dry yeast
2 teaspoons vanilla extract
4 large eggs, at room temperature
2 cups unbleached enriched white flour
1 teaspoon salt
½ cup unsaturated oil, at room temperature

grated zest of 1 lemon
grated zest of 1 orange
juice of 1 medium orange (about ⅜ cup)
½ cup wheat germ
4½ cups unbleached enriched white flour (additional)
2 tablespoons finely chopped nuts

Combine the water and honey, and stir until the honey is dissolved. Add the yeast and stir. Allow to stand for a few minutes, until some yeast action begins.

Measure the vanilla and eggs into a large bowl, beat briefly, then pour the yeast mixture in and stir well.

Add the 2 cups of flour and the salt, stir together, and then beat with an electric mixer for about 5 minutes (or about 10 minutes by hand), until the flour is quite elastic.

Beat in the oil, then the zests, the orange juice, and the wheat germ.

With a wooden spoon, stir in 3½ cups of additional flour, ½ cup at a time.

Spread ¼ cup of flour on the kneading board, scrape the batter onto it, sprinkle ¼ cup over the batter, and then begin to knead.

Knead for about 8 minutes, working in as much of the additional ½ cup flour as required to make a soft, smooth, moist dough. To avoid adding too much flour, in the last stages of kneading flour your hands lightly rather than adding flour to the dough.

Pour about 1 tablespoon of oil into the bottom of the scraped-out mixing bowl, put in the dough, and turn to oil all sides. Then set to rise, covered with a dry towel, in a warm, draft-free place, until the dough has doubled and passes the finger test (see page 6)—about 1½ to 2 hours.

Grease a bundt pan well, and sprinkle the finely chopped nuts over the entire inside.

When risen, punch the dough down and knead it gently and briefly in the bowl to get rid of any large bubbles.

Shape into a thick roll, join the ends, and fit into the bundt pan.

Cover with a dry towel and return to the warm place to rise for about an hour.

Preheat your oven to 375°F. and bake for about 45 minutes, or until the bread tests done (see page 7).

Allow to cool briefly in the pan, then turn out onto a wire rack to cool.

Mandelbrot

Mandelbrot means almond bread, but there is more to this bread than that. It is a delicious and different "twice-baked" Jewish dessert bread.

◊ *Almond paste can be found in some supermarkets (usually in the imported foods section), but we buy it from a local bakery.*
◊ *We use raisins instead of the more traditional candied citron.*

MAKES 2 LOAVES IN SLICES

3 cups unbleached enriched white flour
¼ cup wheat germ
2 teaspoons baking powder
¼ teaspoon salt
½ cup unsulfured raisins
3 large eggs, at room temperature

¾ cup honey
½ teaspoon vanilla extract
1 teaspoon almond extract
2 tablespoons unsaturated oil
1 cup almond paste
4 teaspoons cinnamon
1 cup almonds, slivered or chopped

In a large bowl, stir together the flour, wheat germ, baking powder, salt, and raisins until well mixed. Set aside.

In another bowl, combine the eggs, honey, extracts, oil, and almond paste, and beat until smooth. If the almond paste is too stiff to beat, combine these ingredients in your blender or food processor and blend.

Pour the wet ingredients into the flour mixture, and stir until everything is moist. The consistency should be almost as dry as a cookie dough. If necessary, stir in another tablespoon or 2 more of flour.

Grease two large cookie sheets.

Preheat your oven to 350°F.

Divide the dough in half, and scrape one half onto one sheet. With your hands, press the dough flat, about ¼ inch thick and almost the length of the sheet. If the dough sticks, flour your hands or the dough lightly.

Sprinkle 1 teaspoon of cinnamon over the flattened dough, and press it in with your hand. Sprinkle ¼ cup of almonds over the cinnamon, and press in with your hand.

Using a scraper to lift the dough, fold one long side over the middle, more than halfway, then the other side.

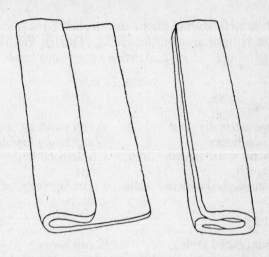

Press down, and keep pressing until you have flattened the dough again, back to about its original shape.

Once again, spread 1 teaspoon of cinnamon over the surface and press it in, then ¼ cup almonds and press them in.

Again, lift the sides and fold the dough into thirds.

Now, shape the loaf to its final form: a mound that runs the length of the sheet, gently rounded at the sides and about 1 inch high. The cinnamon on your hands acts a little like flour here to keep the dough from sticking.

Repeat for the second loaf.

Bake for about 20 minutes, then remove. Note: It is not quite done yet.

Quickly, using a towel to protect your hand from the heat, slice across the loaves, making slices about ½-inch thick.

Lay the slices on their sides, return the sheets to the oven, and continue to bake, turning once, until the slices are golden—about 5 minutes per side.

Cool the slices on a wire rack.

Kolasch

Kolasch are Hungarian poppy-seed-topped buns (the name comes from the Hungarian word for circle). Though the filling is sweet, the dough is not, which makes these yeast buns lovely for breakfast.

MAKES 20 BUNS

The Dough:

1 package active dry yeast
¼ teaspoon honey
1 cup warm water (about 110°F., see page 9)
5 cups unbleached enriched white flour

⅓ cup unsaturated oil
⅓ cup honey (additional)
1 tablespoon freshly grated lemon zest
3 extra-large eggs, at room temperature

The Filling:

¾ cup unsulfured raisins
½ cup warm water (about 110°F.)
½ cup poppy seeds

½ cup honey
1 teaspoon ground allspice
2 tablespoons lemon juice.

In a large bowl, mix together the yeast, the ¼ teaspoon honey, warm water, and 1 cup of the flour, and allow to stand for a few minutes, until yeast action begins.

Add the oil, the ⅓ cup honey, the zest, the eggs, and about 3 cups of flour, and mix thoroughly. Mound the remaining cup of flour onto the side of the kneading board to be worked in during the kneading. You want a soft dough—with just enough flour not to be sticky. Still, it will probably take a good 10 minutes of easy kneading to develop elasticity.

When the dough is bouncy, pour about 1 tablespoon of oil into a large clean bowl. Put in the dough, and turn it over once to oil the surface.

Cover with a dry towel and set in a warm, draft-free place to rise for a couple of hours, until it passes the finger test (page 6).

Meanwhile, begin the filling: Combine all the ingredients in a saucepan and allow to stand so that the raisins and seeds absorb some of the liquid.

Grease two large baking sheets.

Punch down the dough, and turn it out onto the kneading board.

Divide the dough in half, then in half again. Divide each quarter into five roughly equal pieces and shape them into balls.

Place the balls on the baking sheets about 3 inches apart (they must have room to be flattened and to spread). Press with your fingers to make circles 2¾ to 3 inches across (they will grow to about 4 inches across during rising and baking).

Cover the baking sheets with dry towels, and set to rise in a warm place, while you complete the preparation of the filling.

Preheat the oven to 375°F.

To complete the filling: Put the saucepan over low heat, and allow the filling to simmer, stirring frequently, until most of the liquid has boiled away (about 12 minutes). Remove from the heat and allow to cool for a few minutes.

When the buns have puffed somewhat, press down into the center of each with the bowl of a soup spoon. Don't go through to the baking sheet, but do press hard enough to make a lasting impression.

Divide the filling among the dough rounds, placing about 2 teaspoons into each depression.

Bake until golden brown—from 12 to 15 minutes. If they bake unevenly, turn them; if some are brown sooner than others, remove them.

Cool briefly on a wire rack, but if possible, serve warm.

Russian Easter Bread (Kulich)

This is a spectacular bread: handsome to look at, delicious to taste.
It is baked in coffee cans to get the traditional shape.

◊ We use dried fruit rather than the customary candied fruit,
and we prefer hazelnuts to the more usual almonds.
◊ Do not omit toasting the nuts—that dries them, makes them
tastier, and keeps them crisper in the baking.
◊ We use Triple Sec, an orange-flavored liqueur, but curaçao or
even rum will do.
◊ If you cannot find dried cherries, use a total of ¾ cup of raisins.
If you cannot find dried mango or papaya, try dried pineapple
and apricot.
◊ A marble board works best for kneading this bread.

MAKES 3 LOAVES IN 1-POUND COFFEE CANS

The Dough:

½ cup unsulfured raisins
¼ cup chopped dried cherries
¼ cup dried mango or papaya
½ cup Triple Sec
½ cup very warm milk (about
115°F., see page 9)
½ cup honey
3 packages active dry yeast
1 cup unbleached enriched white
flour

1 teaspoon salt
4 large eggs, at room temperature
½ cup unsaturated oil, at room
temperature
2 teaspoons vanilla extract
grated zest of 1 lemon
¼ cup wheat germ
3¾ cups unbleached enriched white
flour (additional)
½ cup hazelnuts

The Glaze:

1 tablespoon lemon juice
1 tablespoon honey

1 tablespoon Triple Sec

Combine the fruit and the Triple Sec, and allow to soak for about
1 hour.

Stir together the warm milk and honey, add the yeast, and stir until well mixed. Allow to stand for a few minutes, until the yeast action begins.

Measure the 1 cup of flour and the salt into a large bowl, then add the yeast mixture and stir well.

Beat for about 7 minutes with an electric mixer (or about 14 minutes by hand) to develop the gluten.

Beat in the eggs well, one at a time.

Beat in the oil, then the vanilla extract, zest, and wheat germ, thoroughly.

Beat in the fruit and Triple Sec.

Add 1 cup of additional flour, ½ cup at a time, beating each for about 1 minute with the electric mixer, or 2 minutes by hand.

Switch over to a wooden spoon and, ½ cup at a time, mix in another 1½ cups of flour.

Sprinkle ¼ cup of flour onto the kneading board, scrape the batter onto it, sprinkle another ¼ cup of flour over the top, and begin to knead, starting out gently.

Knead for about 6 minutes, adding as much as required of the remaining ¾ cup of flour to make a smooth, moist dough.

Pour about 1 tablespoon of oil into the scraped-out mixing bowl, put in the dough, and turn it over to oil all sides.

Cover with a dry towel and set to rise in a warm, draft-free place for about 2 hours, or until the dough has at least doubled in volume and passes a finger test (see page 6).

Meanwhile, coarsely chop (quarter) the hazelnuts, place them in a dry skillet, and toast for about 4 minutes over medium heat, tossing frequently, until lightly browned.

Grease very well three 1-pound (*not* 13-ounce) coffee cans.

When risen, punch down the dough. Sprinkle the cooled nuts over the dough, and knead briefly in the bowl, until the nuts are well distributed through the dough. You may have to dust your hands with flour a few times to knead easily.

Cut the dough into three parts; round each part into a ball and put it into a coffee can.

Set to rise, covered with a dry towel, for about 1 hour, or until doubled in volume.

Starting in a cold oven set for 375°F., bake for about 40 minutes, or until the loaves test done (see page 7).

Knock the loaves out of the cans and place upright onto a platter.

To glaze the bread: Combine the lemon juice, honey, and Triple

Sec and stir well; brush generously all over the hot loaves with a pastry brush.

To serve this bread in the traditional manner, cut the mushroom-caplike top off a glazed and cooled loaf and place it in the center of a round platter; cut the remainder of the loaf in half vertically, then slice both halves into ½-inch semicircles. Arrange the slices around the cap, like petals around the center of a flower. Serve the other loaves similarly, or store them in the freezer.

Hot Cross Buns

These are a traditional English Easter treat—and, as you might guess, they are best served hot from the oven.

◊ *If you have no pastry bag for the icing, shape a cornet (page 236) out of baker's parchment—or even waxed paper.*

MAKES ABOUT 20 BUNS

The Dough:

1 package active dry yeast
1¼ cups hot nonfat milk (about 125°F., see page 9)
¼ cup honey
¼ cup unsaturated oil
½ teaspoon salt
1 teaspoon vanilla extract
1 teaspoon ground cinnamon
1 large egg, at room temperature

zest of ½ lemon
2 cups unbleached enriched white flour
¼ cup unsulfured raisins
¼ cup chopped dates
¼ cup wheat germ
1¼ to 1½ cups unbleached enriched white flour (additional)

The Icing:

4 ounces cream cheese

2 to 3 tablespoons honey

In a large bowl, dissolve the yeast in the hot milk, stir in the honey, and the oil.

Add the salt, vanilla, cinnamon, and egg, and grate in the lemon zest. Mix with an electric mixer at medium-low speed (or by hand) until fairly smooth.

Add the 2 cups of flour a bit at a time, and beat at medium speed for 5 minutes (about 10 minutes by hand), until the batter is fairly elastic.

Stir in the wheat germ and the dried fruit with a wooden spoon.

Stir in 1 cup of the additional flour.

Sprinkle ¼ cup of flour on the kneading board, scrape the dough out onto it, sprinkle another ¼ cup of flour on top, and knead gently.

Knead until the dough is cohesive but somewhat loose, adding as much of the remaining flour as necessary, but no more.

Pour a teaspoon of oil into the scraped-out mixing bowl, put in the dough, and turn it to oil all sides.

Cover with a dry towel and set in a warm, draft-free place to rise for about 1¼ hours, or until it passes the finger test (see page 6).

Dust the board lightly with flour, and scrape out the dough onto it.

Grease a large cookie sheet.

Preheat your oven to 375°F.

Tear off egg-sized lumps of dough, roll them between your palms to make balls, and place them in five rows of four on the sheet. Flatten each slightly, and set to rise, covered with a dry towel, for about 20 minutes, or until visibly risen.

Bake for about 17 minutes, or until the bottoms are browned and one or two buns pass a toothpick test (page 7).

To make the icing: Combine the cream cheese and 2 tablespoons of the honey and beat with a fork until smooth. Taste, and add the last tablespoon of honey if desired.

Spoon the icing into a small pastry bag with an ⅛-inch tip and, while the buns are still hot, mark the top of each with a cross of white icing.

Serve warm.

Italian Easter Bread (Cresca)

Here is a beauty of a festive dinner bread from northern Italy. One loaf is about enough for a family of four or five, and it slices beautifully.

◊ *For a larger party, double the recipe and bake two loaves.*
◊ *This is a stiff dough and so it requires a lot of kneading, and a lot of rising time.*
◊ *You might wish to sift the grated cheese—that will save a lot of stirring.*

MAKES 1 9-INCH ROUND BREAD

1 package active dry yeast
⅜ cup warm milk (about 110°F., see page 9)
3 large eggs, at room temperature
2 tablespoons olive oil
1 cup unbleached enriched white flour

¼ cup bran
¼ cup wheat germ
1 tablespoon coarse-ground black pepper
1 cup grated Parmesan cheese
2½ cups unbleached enriched white flour (additional)

Dissolve the yeast in the milk in a large bowl, add the eggs and the oil, and beat until well mixed.

Add the 1 cup of flour and beat with an electric mixer at medium speed for about 5 minutes (or about 10 minutes by hand)—until the batter is elastic.

Stir in the bran and wheat germ, then the pepper and grated Parmesan cheese.

Add 1 cup of the additional flour and beat vigorously with a wooden spoon for a few seconds.

Spread ¼ cup of flour on the board, scrape the batter onto it, and spread another cup of flour over the top.

Knead well for about 10 minutes, working in as much of the remaining flour as you can (making a total of about 3½ cups of flour). The finished dough will stand on its own, without spreading, and not be sticky at all.

Put a tablespoon of olive oil into the scraped-out mixing bowl, add the dough, and turn it to oil all sides.

Cover with a dry towel and set to rise in a warm, draft-free place for about two hours, or until the volume of the dough has doubled and it passes a finger test (see page 6).

Punch down and rise again for about an hour, or until you see the same doubling.

Grease a 9-inch round cake pan well.

Scrape the dough onto the board, knead it down gently, and flatten it to make a domed disk that covers most of the bottom of the cake pan.

Set to rise in a warm place, covered with a dry towel, for about 1½ hours. Again, you should see ample rising.

Starting in a cold oven set for 350°F., bake for about 1 hour. The loaf should be browned and should test done (see page 7).

Cool on a wire rack but serve while still warm.

Challah

Challah is the traditional braided Jewish Sabbath loaf. The challah one sees in bakeries is most often made from six strands of dough— one quarter of the dough made into a small braid of three strands, set atop a larger braid of three strands made from the remaining three quarters of the dough.

But to have a loaf symbolic of the Sabbath, you need seven strands (one strand for each day of the week): a small three atop a large three, interwoven with or crowned by a single strand, signifying the Sabbath—the crown of the week.

However, the number of strands does not affect the flavor and texture of this very satisfying bread.

Challah dough is a pleasure to handle. The combination of oil and eggs gives it a silky feel, and makes it so easy to work with that children can participate in the kneading and braiding.

This bread is a fine keeper, so you don't have to worry about having an extra loaf around for a few days.

◇ *Don't skimp on the kneading just because the dough feels so nice so quickly.*

◇ *If the day is really damp, decrease the water in the recipe by about ⅛ cup. Otherwise, the loaf will accept extra flour and could come out a bit dry and less sweet.*

◇ *Form the braids as soon as you have made the strands, or they may dry and come apart in the baking. However, if you do have to leave the strands for as little as 10 minutes, moisten your fingertips with water when you come back, and lightly wet the strands—especially at the ends where you tuck them under.*

◇ *A marble kneading board works best for Challah.*

◇ *For a more nutritious loaf, substitute 1 cup of wheat germ for an equal amount of flour. The wheat germ makes for a nuttier flavor.*

◇ *Challah makes the best French toast we know.*

MAKES 2 LOAVES

The Dough:

2 packages active dry yeast
4 teaspoons salt
¾ cup honey, at room temperature
1¾ cups hot water (about 125°F., see page 9)
2 cups unbleached enriched white flour

1¼ cups unsaturated oil, at room temperature
3 large eggs, at room temperature
5 to 6 cups unbleached enriched white flour (additional)

The Glaze:

1 large egg

1 to 2 tablespoons poppy seeds

Measure the yeast, salt, honey, and hot water into a large bowl and stir.

Mix in the 2 cups of flour, the oil, and the eggs.

Add 4 more cups of additional flour, 1 cup at a time, beating each cup in well with a wooden spoon. When the stirring gets difficult, clean the spoon into the bowl (see page 11), and mix with your bare hand.

Sprinkle ¼ cup of flour onto the kneading board and scrape the dough onto it. Knead in enough of the remaining flour as necessary to make a dough that is silky and resilient, but still soft. Don't force in every last bit of flour that you can—this dough must remain silky.

After you have reached that silky state, 8 to 10 minutes of additional kneading should bring out the faint wrinkles on the surface that signify sufficient kneading (see page 3).

Pour about 1 tablespoon of oil into the scraped-out mixing bowl, put in the dough, and turn it to oil all sides.

Cover with a dry towel and set to rise in a very warm, draft-free place for about 1 hour, until it passes the finger test (see page 6). The dough should more than double in volume—a full first rise is vital to challah.

Punch the dough down in the bowl, turn it out onto the board, and knead for a minute to squeeze out the larger bubbles. Shape into a mound.

Grease a large baking sheet.

Cut the mound of dough in half for two loaves. For three-strand loaves, cut each half into three equal pieces.

Do not roll the strands on your board. Using your hands and gravity, squeeze and roll each of the three pieces of dough into a "rope" about 1 inch thick, and lay them on the board side by side, but not touching, to be braided.

Begin braiding in the middle as illustrated on page 66, and braid overhand down to the end. Tuck the ends under and give them a little pinch to close them off.

Turn your board and braid underhand down to the other end, and tuck the ends under and pinch closed. (Braiding this way yields a more symmetrical loaf.)

Transfer the braid to the baking sheet, leaving room for the second loaf.

Braid the second loaf and transfer to the sheet. Leave room in between: These loaves will rise and spread a lot.

Cover with a dry towel and return them to that warm, draft-free place to rise for about ½ hour (or more), until the loaves look well risen.

To glaze the loaves: Break an egg into a cup and beat it lightly with a fork. With your fingers or a pastry brush, spread the egg gently over the visible parts of both loaves, and sprinkle poppy seeds over the tops.

Put into the middle of a cold oven set for 350°F., and bake for about 50 minutes, or until a toothpick thrust between the thickest of the braids comes out clean. When done, the bottom color should be a rich reddish brown.

Cool briefly on a wire rack, then serve warm, tearing pieces off. Do not slice until cool.

BRIOCHES

Imagine a bread lighter than challah, with a pastry-like texture, a crisp crust that literally melts as you chew it, and a taste that has to be experienced to be believed.

From the same dough we make three kinds of brioches: Brioche rolls cook up perfectly well in muffin trays, though if you have tart molds with fluted sides, the flutings add character to the shape. Topknot brioche is usually baked as a freestanding loaf on a baking sheet, but it can also be baked in a straight-sided mold or a 2-pound coffee can. Crown brioche requires a ring mold.

Or, if you like, you can braid the dough, or bake it in shaped pans, or put it on a sheet in whatever new shape you wish to invent.

    ◇ *This dough is the best riser in the book, nearly tripling in volume.*

    ◇ *Don't flour your hands when you are handling the dough—either for shaping or working out the air bubbles after rising. The additional flour coarsens the texture.*

    ◇ *Hot whole milk can be substituted for the nonfat milk powder and hot water.*

    ◇ *For a brighter flavor, add the grated zest of 1 lemon.*

    ◇ *For a more nutritious brioche, substitute up to 1 cup of wheat germ for an equal amount of flour. But if you do, you'll have to grease the pans or molds or sheets: The flecks of wheat germ tend to stick.*

    ◇ *Because of the oiliness of brioche, the uneaten portion should be refrigerated.*

Brioche

The Brioche:

2 packages active dry yeast
¼ cup honey, at room temperature
1 teaspoon salt
½ cup hot water (about 125°F., see page 9)
½ cup nonfat milk powder
1 cup unbleached enriched white flour

1 cup unsaturated oil, at room temperature
4½ large eggs (4 whole eggs + 1 egg white), at room temperature
4 cups unbleached enriched white flour (additional)

The Glaze:

1 egg yolk

1 teaspoon water

Measure the yeast, honey, salt, and water into a large bowl, and stir.

Mix in the milk powder and the 1 cup of flour.

Add the oil and eggs (reserving the leftover yolk for the glaze). Beat with a whisk until quite smooth.

Begin to stir in the additional 4 cups of flour, 1 cup at a time. When whisking becomes too much like work, clean the dough out from the whisk (see page 11) and work with your hands.

Continuing to work in the bowl, knead in the remaining flour until your hands come clean and the dough shapes readily into a large ball. Add no more flour, but continue to knead for about 10 minutes, until the dough wrinkles (see page 3).

Cover the bowl with a dry towel and put in a very warm, draft-free place to rise for about 1½ hours, until it almost triples in volume and passes the finger test (see page 6).

Punch down, knead for a minute in the bowl, and shape.

Brioche Rolls (*Petites Brioches*)

MAKES 24 ROLLS

Reserving about one fifth of the risen and kneaded dough for the tops, shape the rest into twenty-four balls about 1½ inches in diameter.

To form each ball, pinch off a bit of dough and either roll it between your palms or use a stretching and tucking motion: Stretch the dough smooth across the top and then tuck the ends into the bottom, repeating until the ball is smooth to the eye. Place the balls, rough side down, into the ungreased cups of muffin pans or tart molds, and dent the tops with a finger.

In the same fashion, shape the reserved dough into twenty-four ¾-inch balls. These balls will sit in the dents on top of the larger balls.

Dip a finger in water, wet a dent, and place a small ball into it. The water acts as a glue to keep these little "heads" on. Repeat until all the balls are in place.

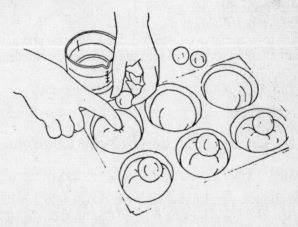

Cover with a dry towel, and rise in a warm place for about 40 minutes, or until about doubled.

To glaze the rolls: Mix the yolk with the water and brush it over the rolls with a pastry brush.

Starting in a cold oven set for 375°F., bake for about 20 minutes, until a toothpick inserted in the neck comes out clean (see page 7).

Cool briefly on a wire rack, or eat right from the pans.

Topknot Brioche (*Brioche à Tête*)

MAKES 2 TOPKNOTS

These are the same shape as the Brioche Rolls—just bigger.

Divide the risen and kneaded-down dough in half.

Reserve about a fifth of each half for the tops. Shape the remaining four fifths of each into a smooth ball with the stretching and tucking technique described and illustrated above for Brioche Rolls.

Place the two balls, rough side down, onto a large, ungreased baking sheet, leaving room for spread. With two fingers, make a dent on top of each.

Shape the two smaller balls, dip two fingers into water, wet the dents, and place a smaller ball into each dent.

Cover with a dry towel and set to rise in a warm, draft-free place for about 40 minutes. (Do not use bottom heat: that will spread the brioches instead of rising them.)

Glaze as described on page 131.

Starting in a cold oven set for 375°F., bake for about 30 minutes, or until a toothpick pushed into the neck comes out clean (see page 7).

Cool on a wire rack, or eat hot from the oven.

Crown Brioche (*Brioche Couronne*)

MAKES 1 VERY LARGE CROWN OR 2 MODERATE-SIZED CROWNS

Shape the risen and punched-down dough into a ball. Using the same stretching and tucking method described on page 131, smooth it on one side.

Poke your finger through from the smooth top to the rough bottom, making a hole. Pick it up and turn it sideways. With gravity as a stretching aid, shake the dough gently and rotate the circle (a big doughnut shape, actually) in your hands, forcing in more fingers to enlarge the hole, until the crown has an outside diameter of about 8 inches.

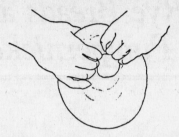

Place the crown on an ungreased baking sheet (or in a tube pan), and make a few final pulls and tucks to get it into a fairly uniform shape.

With a clean large pair of scissors, clip eight to twelve slashes evenly into the top of the crown, about a third of the way through. This will encourage it to rise up. If you want it to rise *out*, clip the sides.

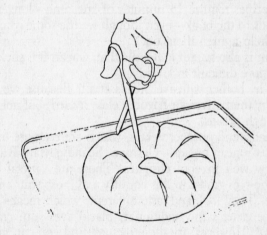

Cover with a dry towel and rise in a warm draft-free place for about 40 minutes, until about doubled.

Glaze as described on page 131.

Starting in a cold oven set for 375°F., bake for 30 to 40 minutes, or until the crown tests done (see page 7).

Cool on a wire rack, or eat hot from the oven.

8

Rye Breads and Pumpernickel

RYE flour is a low-gluten flour, so one does have to work like blazes to develop the elasticity that enables it to hold a rise. Three of these recipes require 15 minutes of kneading—longer than any other breads in the book—even though we use some wheat in every recipe to help lighten them up.

Rye flour is also harder to handle than wheat. It is stickier, which makes it more difficult to knead.

Then why bother with rye breads at all? Because rye breads are in a class by themselves for flavor (a class rivaled, but not surpassed, by sourdough breads).

Rye breads (and pumpernickels, which are ryes) are traditionally northern European breads—German, Scandinavian, Russian. The grains grow well in cool climates. There are varietal differences between the ryes grown in this country and those your ancestors ate in Europe. They look and taste different, which means we cannot make those exact same traditional "black" ryes your grandparents raved about. However, try these recipes, and you can rave to *your* grandchildren.

Rye doughs tend to "draw wet." That means that even when the bread is baked enough to eat, it may still show streaking on the knife blade when you test it for doneness (see page 7). Tapping the loaf on its bottom will give you a satisfying hollow sound when the loaf is done. Test with the knife first, but if it draws out a few streaks of moisture (not dough), thump for confirmation.

Yes, this sounds inexact, but a lot of baking is like that.

You can always cut a loaf open and then, if the loaf is not baked through, press the cut ends back together and bake longer. No, the cut won't heal, but the loaf will finish baking.

More than other breads, ryes like an occasional flouring of the kneading board—even after "enough" flour is in.

Also, you'll have to clean your hands of dough more often. Sprinkle a little flour on your palms and rub away as much dough as you can, spilling it onto the dough ball. Take a spoon and scrape away what remains.

Are you discouraged? Don't be. These are rewarding breads, healthful and great tasting.

◊ *Share the kneading of these breads with a friend. If you have no one to help, knead in spurts, covering the dough with the inverted mixing bowl while you rest. The dough doesn't care whether you knead in five 3-minute chunks or one 15-minute sprint. If you own a dough hook or a food processor, these are the breads where their help is appreciated.*

◊ *Here is something we have found helpful in baking rye breads. If the bottoms of the loaves are showing signs of getting burnt before the loaf tests done, turn the loaves over and let them bake for the last few minutes topside down.*

Potato Rye

Potato Rye (and Swedish Rye, which follows) should be rated "X"—
for adults only; the flavors are too definite for kids.

This is an old, traditional bread, with European roots. The potato
helps to solidify the texture, making for a satisfying, crusty, heavy
(though by no means too heavy) bread.

This bread is not a high riser. It is higher than an all-rye bread
would be, but only two thirds as high as most other loaves we've
been making. But that's the nature of rye.

◇ *Potato water is a great yeast feeder. Whenever you boil potatoes,
  save the water for bread baking.*
◇ *Both the potatoes and the water should be hot: 125° to 140°F.
  If you use them cold, it will slow down the rising by hours.*
◇ *For a more nutritious loaf substitute ¼ cup of wheat germ or
  bran for part of the rye flour.*
◇ *You could make the recipe easier to handle (but less nutritious)
  by substituting unbleached enriched white flour for all or part
  of the whole wheat. If you do, be sure to substitute ½ cup of
  wheat germ for ½ cup of the rye flour.*
◇ *The kind and amount of seeds you use are very much a matter
  of taste. You may want to try Russian caraway seeds or fennel.*
◇ *If you wish, sprinkle a teaspoon of seeds over each loaf after
  the first spraying.*

MAKES 2 LOAVES

2 packages active dry yeast
1 tablespoon salt
1 tablespoon caraway seeds
2 cups hot potato water (about 125°F., see page 9)

1 packed cup hot mashed potatoes
4 cups whole rye flour
2 to 2½ cups whole wheat flour
2 tablespoons yellow cornmeal

Into a large mixing bowl, measure the yeast, salt, seeds, potato
water, and potatoes. Stir quite well.

Stir in the rye flour, 1 cup at a time.

With a wooden spoon, beat in 1 cup of the whole wheat flour.

Spread 1 cup of whole wheat flour over the kneading board, scrape the batter onto it, turn the batter over, and begin to work the flour in.

Knead for about 15 minutes, adding as much of the remaining ½ cup of whole wheat flour as required to keep your hands and the board moderately free of dough. This dough will never get really dry.

If, after 15 minutes of kneading, you do not feel resistance when you knead, then knead for another 5 minutes. It is important to develop all the gluten possible.

When the dough shows good resistance, stop and scrape your hands clean. Press the scraped bits onto the dough ball.

Pour about 1 teaspoon of oil into the scraped-out mixing bowl, drop in the dough, and turn a few times to oil all sides.

Cover with a clean, hot, wet towel, and set to rise in a quite-warm, draft-free place for 1½ to 2 hours. Because rye dough is low in gluten, the finger test will not tell you when this dough is risen, so look for it to be about doubled in bulk.

Grease a large baking sheet and sprinkle with the cornmeal. Shake and tap the sheet to distribute the cornmeal evenly.

When the dough is risen, punch it down, and gently knead in the bowl for a moment to get rid of the larger bubbles.

Scrape the dough onto the kneading board and cut in half.

Knead each half into a smooth ball, then shape into a loaf about 4 by 8 inches and as high as you can.

Lay the loaves on the sheet, spaced well apart. With a sharp knife, make three or four diagonal slashes, evenly spaced down each loaf, to a depth of about ½ inch.

Cover with a dry towel, and set to rise for 45 minutes to an hour (about half the time of the first rise). The slashes will gape wide when the loaves are risen, and the loaves themselves will look considerably larger. (If you are not sure, rise some more.)

When risen, spray the loaves with tepid water to help get that marvelous crunchy crust. Spray again after 15 minutes of baking.

Starting in a cold oven set at 375°F., bake for 50 minutes, then shut off the heat and leave in the hot oven for another 10 minutes. Thump the bottom of the loaf: if it sounds hollow, it's done.

Cool on a wire rack for ½ hour, then eat warm.

Swedish Rye

Swedish Rye is definitely the tastiest rye in the book—perhaps even too savory for breakfast.

This is a traditional Swedish bread—but made with nutritious blackstrap molasses instead of sugary corn syrup—and quite different from most of the other kneaded breads we make.

Instead of slashing the loaves, we will repeatedly prick the surface of the shaped loaves with a fork.

Instead of working for a crisp crust, we will brush the loaf with milk to get a soft crust. (If you prefer a hard crust to a soft one, spray twice with water, as in Potato Rye, page 136).

Instead of the usual shapes for whole-grain breads, we will shape this dough like French baguettes.

◊ *When you shape the loaves, give the individual thirds a good kneading and form them into smooth balls before you roll them out to the long loaves. If there are folds in the dough, they will not disappear in the baking.*

◊ *If you wish, substitute another liquid for the potato water called for: skim milk or buttermilk are very Scandinavian; beer is a popular liquid in ryes; the water left after boiling vegetables is fine. Whatever liquid you use, heat it to about 125°F. If you do not use potato water, increase the salt by 1 teaspoon.*

◊ *Don't eliminate the oil: It makes this dough much easier to handle.*

◊ *Don't use ground fennel (unless you are desperate—in which case, use only 1½ tablespoons).*

◊ *The taste of the fennel-seed-and-orange combination is super, but anise seed is also appropriate. Crush it in the same way.*

◊ *For an even more nutritious bread, substitute ½ cup of wheat germ or bran for ½ cup of the rye flour.*

Makes 3 Loaves

2 tablespoons fennel seed	grated zest of 1 orange
2 packages active dry yeast	¼ cup unsaturated oil
¼ cup blackstrap molasses	3 cups whole rye flour
¼ cup honey	3½ to 4 cups whole wheat flour
2 cups hot potato water (about 125°F., see page 9)	¼ cup yellow cornmeal
	tepid milk
2 teaspoons salt	

In a large bowl, crush the fennel seed with the back of the bowl of a strong spoon.

Add the yeast, molasses, honey, and potato water. Stir well.

Stir in the salt, zest, and oil.

With a wooden spoon, beat in the rye flour, 1 cup at a time.

Mix in 3 cups of the whole wheat flour, 1 cup at a time.

Spread ½ cup of whole wheat flour over the kneading board, scrape the batter onto it, and work the flour in.

Knead for 15 minutes, using as much of the remaining ½ cup of whole wheat as necessary to keep the dough from sticking to your hands and the board. Try not to go beyond that fourth cup of whole wheat, but dust your hands as required.

When well kneaded (the dough will be springy), pour a teaspoon of oil into the scraped-out mixing bowl, put in the dough, and turn it a few times to oil all sides. Cover with a hot, wet towel, and set in a very warm, draft-free place to rise for about 1½ hours. Because rye doughs are low in gluten, the finger test will not tell you when this dough is risen, so look for it to double in volume.

When risen, punch down the dough, and knead in the bowl for a moment to get rid of the larger bubbles.

Grease two large baking sheets, and sprinkle with cornmeal, tilting and tapping the sheet to make an even, thin layer.

Turn the dough onto the board and cut into three pieces. Shape the dough into three smooth balls. Roll the balls with your hands into long loaves, about 2 by 14 inches. Dust your hands frequently with whole wheat flour to keep the dough from sticking.

Lay two on one sheet, one on the other. Prick all over the surfaces with a fork, about ⅛ to ¼ inch deep.

Cover with a dry towel, and set in a warm, draft-free place to rise for 30 to 45 minutes. The loaves should look considerably risen, though not doubled.

With a pastry brush, brush the tops very gently with the milk. Be careful: These loaves are easy to knock down. (If you used beer as a liquid in the dough, brush with beer.

Starting in a cold oven set for 375°F., bake for about 30 minutes, or until the bread tests done (see page 7), either with a knife or with the hollow sound when you tap the bottom of the loaves.

Cool on a wire rack for a few minutes, and serve hot.

Refrigerator Rye

If Potato Rye and Swedish Rye are rated "for adults only," here is a rye bread rated "G." This bread is milder flavored than most ryes, and made in loaf pans for a sandwich shape, both of which children like.

◊ *If this is your first experience with a refrigerator-rise bread, you might want to refer to Chapter 3, where the method is discussed.*

◊ *You can substitute dark molasses for the blackstrap. The bread will not have as much nutritional value and will have a milder flavor.*

◊ *For more calcium, add ¾ cup of skim milk powder (no other adjustment to the recipe is needed), or substitute hot milk for the water.*

◊ *Any vegetable water is a welcome substitution for the water.*

◊ *For interest, add 1 tablespoon of caraway, fennel, or anise seeds to the mixing bowl—or knead in 1 teaspoon of seeds when shaping each loaf.*

◊ *For a more nutritious bread, substitute ½ cup of bran or wheat germ for ½ cup of rye flour.*

MAKES 3 LOAVES IN 8-INCH PANS

2 packages active dry yeast
1 tablespoon salt
⅓ cup blackstrap molasses
¼ cup unsaturated oil
2 cups hot water (about 125°F., see page 9)

3 cups whole rye flour
3 to 3½ cups unbleached enriched white flour

Grease well three 8-inch loaf pans.

In a large mixing bowl, combine the yeast, salt, molasses, oil, and water. Stir well.

Beat in the rye flour, 1 cup at a time.

Beat in 2 cups of the white flour, 1 cup at a time.

Spread 1 cup of white flour over the kneading board, scrape the batter onto it, and work the flour in.

Knead in as much of the remaining ½ cup of white flour as required to make the dough handleable. Knead for another 10 minutes, dusting your hands and the board as necessary. The dough is ready when it is quite cohesive and springy. Divide the dough into three equal pieces, form each piece into a loaf shape, and put a loaf into each pan.

With your fingers, level out the surfaces.

Grease three pieces of plastic wrap well, loosely cover each loaf, and set in the refrigerator in a place where they will have room to rise well above the pans.

Allow to rise undisturbed for 6 to 12 hours.

When you are ready to bake, gently take the loaves out of the refrigerator and carefully remove the plastics. Do not touch the dough. Put immediately into a cold oven set at 375°F., and bake for about 45 minutes, or until the loaves test done (see page 7).

Turn the loaves out of the pans and cool well on a wire rack for best slicing.

Pumpernickel

This traditional bread is of German origin and combines rye, whole wheat, and white flours in a chewy, flavorful loaf that is a fine keeper.

Occasionally you see a "pumpernickel flour" offered for sale. That's a laugh—there is no pumpernickel plant. It will be a mixture of two or more flours.

We use blackstrap molasses and Postum (a roasted-cereal beverage powder) to get that "black" bread look.

If you can't find Postum, use some other coffee substitute from a health food store; if you use decaffeinated coffee instead, use only 2 level teaspoons in the bread and 1 teaspoon for the glaze. (It's better than the caramel coloring or burnt bread crumbs some recipes use.)

◊ *Pumpernickel is usually made in oval or round free-standing loaves, but you can use three 7½-inch loaf pans instead.*

◊ *We don't slash or prick our pumpernickel loaves because we want them to be dense. If you want a lighter loaf, slash the shaped loaves as with Potato Rye, above.*

◊ *If you forget to glaze before the loaf goes into the oven, glaze it any time up to the last 10 minutes of baking.*

◊ *For interest, use 1 tablespoon of caraway, anise, dill, or fennel seeds in the mixing bowl, or knead 1 teaspoon of seeds into each loaf as you shape it.*

◊ *Substitute any hot liquid for the water: milk, beer, vegetable water.*

◊ *For a more nutritious bread, substitute ¾ cup wheat germ or bran for ¼ cup of each flour.*

◊ *Yellow cornmeal is also acceptable for sprinkling, though white is traditonal.*

MAKES 3 LOAVES

The Dough:

3 packages active dry yeast
2 teaspoons salt
¼ cup blackstrap molasses
1 tablespoon Postum
2 cups hot water (about 125°F., see page 9)

¼ cup unsaturated oil
2 cups whole rye flour
2 cups whole wheat flour
1 to 2 cups unbleached enriched white flour
2 to 3 tablespoons white cornmeal

The Glaze:

1 teaspoon Postum

2 teaspoons hot water

In a large mixing bowl, combine the yeast, salt, molasses, Postum, and hot water. Stir well.

Stir in the oil.

With a wooden spoon, beat in the rye flour, 1 cup at a time, then the whole wheat flour, 1 cup at a time.

Spread 1 cup of the white flour over the kneading board, scrape the batter onto it, and work the flour in.

Knead for 15 minutes, working in as much of the remaining cup of white flour as necessary to stop the dough from sticking and until it is quite resilient.

When kneaded (see page 1), pour a teaspoon of oil into the scraped-out mixing bowl, put in the dough, and turn it a few times to oil all sides.

Cover with a hot, wet towel, and set in a very warm, draft-free place to rise for 1 to 1½ hours, or until it passes the finger test (see page 6). Yes, the finger test works for this "rye."

Grease two large baking sheets, and dust them with white cornmeal, tilting and tapping the sheets to make an even, thin layer.

When the dough has risen, dust your hands with white flour, punch down the dough, and knead it gently for a minute in the bowl to get rid of the larger bubbles.

Scrape the dough onto the kneading board and cut into three equal pieces. Shape each piece into a loaf—round or oval.

Place two loaves on one sheet (leaving plenty of room for rise) and one loaf on the other.

Cover with a dry towel, and set again in that warm, draft-free place to rise for ½ to ¾ hour.

To glaze the loaves: Mix the Postum with the hot water and gently brush onto the surfaces of the loaves with a pastry brush. Be careful not to punch down the loaves.

Starting in a cold oven set at 375°F., bake for 50 to 60 minutes. If the loaves seem close to scorching on their bottoms after 50 minutes, but a tap still doesn't sound hollow and a knife test still brings out dough (see page 7), shut the oven off for the last 10 minutes of baking.

Allow to cool on a wire rack, then serve warm.

≈≈9≈≈

Other Special Grain Breads

THE breads in this chapter are quite exciting for the adventurous baker. The flours used are unusual as major ingredients in breads, and you won't find most of them on supermarket shelves, so you may have to explore the wilds of health food stores. But they are worth the search, because they all add a special something (flavor, texture, nutritional plus) to bread.

For example, cornmeal is slightly sweet and especially tasty. Buckwheat flour has a distinctively strong flavor. Soy flour is very high in quality protein. And they are all rich in fiber.

For more recipes that are all or part "special" grains, see the chapter on rye breads, muffins, and batter breads, and the recipes for Oatmeal Refrigerator Rise, Sour Pumpernickel, Sour Rye, Tortillas, Corn Dodger, Boston Brown Bread, and Blueberry Rice Bread.

◊ *If you find your yeast-risen special-grain breads coming out too dense and heavy, give the dough an extra rise in the bowl next time you try.*

Seven-Grain Bread

Here is a delicious and remarkably light bread with an excellent texture. It can serve as a "sampler" of special grains, because it uses two wheat flours, two cornmeals, buckwheat, rye, barley, rice, and rolled oats.

◊ *Since most of the elasticity to rise this bread is going to have to come from the wheat flours, we beat them separately as a batter for quite a while. Do not stint on this beating. When the elasticity is sufficiently developed, the batter will have a very cohesive and rubbery appearance.*

MAKES 2 LOAVES IN 7½-INCH PANS

2 packages active dry yeast
1¼ cups hot water (about 125°F., see page 9)
¼ cup dark molasses
1½ cups unbleached enriched white flour
1 teaspoon salt
1 cup whole wheat flour
¼ cup whole rye flour

¼ cup buckwheat flour
¼ cup barley flour
¼ cup brown rice flour
¼ cup rolled oats
¼ cup yellow cornmeal
4 to 6 tablespoons unbleached enriched white flour (additional)
2 tablespoons white cornmeal
1 tablespoon caraway seeds

Combine the yeast, water, and molasses in a large mixing bowl. Stir well, and allow to stand for about 10 minutes, until some foam is visible.

Stir in the white and whole wheat flours, and beat with an electric mixer for 6 to 7 minutes (or about 12 minutes by hand) until very elastic.

Cover the bowl with a dry towel and put this batter to rise in a very warm, draft-free place until at least doubled, about 1 hour. Do not finger test; there is no need to. This is a sponge and we don't finger-test sponges.

With a wooden spoon, one at a time, beat in the rye flour, buckwheat flour, barley flour, rice flour, rolled oats, and yellow cornmeal. The batter will be very stiff.

Sprinkle 2 tablespoons of the additional white flour onto the kneading board, scrape the batter onto it, turn the batter over, and begin to knead gently.

Knead for about 4 minutes, dusting with as much of the remaining white flour as you require to keep your hands from sticking. The dough will be light, but quite springy.

Pour about 1 tablespoon of oil into the scraped-out mixing bowl, put in the dough, and turn it to oil all sides.

Cover with a warm, wet towel and set to rise in a very warm, draft-free place, until the dough has doubled and passes the finger test (see page 6), about 30 minutes.

Grease two 7½-inch loaf pans, pour 1 tablespoon of white corn-meal into each, and tip and tap to cover all the insides of the pans with a thin, even layer of cornmeal. Pour off the excess.

When the dough is risen, sprinkle the caraway seeds over the surface, then punch it down and knead in the seeds. You may need to dust your hands with white flour as you knead.

Cut the dough in half. Form into loaves, and put one into each pan.

Set to rise in a very warm, draft-free place, covered with a dry towel until the dough fills the pans—10 to 15 minutes.

Starting in a cold oven set at 375°F., bake for 30 minutes, or until the loaves test done (see page 7).

Turn the loaves out of the pans and cool on a wire rack before slicing.

Buckwheat Sandwich Loaf

Buckwheat is a strong-flavored flour, of little gluten, which is usually used in pancakes, not bread. (Buckwheat pancakes often have a grayish look.) But here is a delicious loaf with mixed grains, good for sandwiches, of excellent texture and flavor, with just enough of the distinctive buckwheat taste.

The pumpkin seeds, and their uneven grinding, give this bread a unique taste and crunch. Shelled pumpkin seeds can be ground briefly in a blender, for the proper texture.

◊ *Because of the potential heaviness of the buckwheat flour, we give this bread a second rise in the bowl.*

MAKES 3 LOAVES IN 7½-INCH PANS

2 packages active dry yeast
2 cups hot water (about 125°F., see page 9)
2 large eggs, at room temperature
¼ cup unsaturated oil
¼ cup honey
1½ teaspoons salt
2 cups unbleached enriched white flour

½ cup shelled pumpkin seeds, coarsely ground
1 cup whole wheat flour
1 cup buckwheat flour
1 cup whole wheat flour (additional)

In a large bowl, dissolve the yeast in the hot water.

Beat in the eggs, oil, honey, and salt.

Add the white flour and beat for 5 minutes (or about 10 minutes by hand) with an electric mixer, at medium-low speed, until it is quite elastic.

Stir in the ground pumpkin seeds.

Add the whole wheat flour, and beat vigorously with a wooden spoon.

Stir in the buckwheat flour. The batter will be quite thick by this time.

Spread ¼ cup of the additional whole wheat flour on the kneading board, scrape the batter onto it, and dust a little flour over the top.

Turn the butter and begin to work in the flour.

Knead for 5 to 8 minutes, adding a total of about ½ cup more whole wheat flour during the kneading, to arrive at a dough that is elastic, but still soft and a little sticky.

Pour about 1 tablespoon of oil into the scraped-out mixing bowl, put in the dough, and turn it until lightly oiled on all sides.

Set to rise, covered with a dry towel, in a warm, draft-free place for about an hour, until it passes the finger test (see page 6).

When risen, punch the dough down in the bowl with a floured hand, and set it back into the warmth, covered with the same towel, for a second rise of about 30 minutes, or until well risen.

Grease three 7½-inch loaf pans well.

When risen, punch the dough down again, and divide it among the three pans. The dough will still be somewhat sticky, and can be spooned into the pans.

Now, put the loaf pans to rise in that same warm place, covered, for only 15 to 20 minutes.

Starting in a cold oven set for 375°F., bake for about 35 minutes, or until the loaves test done (see page 7).

Turn the loaves out of the pans and cool on a wire rack before slicing.

Granola Breakfast Spiral

This is a sweet and savory bread—though how sweet depends on your granola. We buy one that is unsweetened.

This is a "breakfast" bread because it evokes childhood memories of cinnamon toast on winter mornings.

MAKES 2 LOAVES IN 8½-INCH PANS

The Dough:

2 packages active dry yeast
2 cups hot water (about 125°F., see page 9)
¼ cup unsaturated oil
¼ cup honey
3 cups unbleached enriched white flour

1½ teaspoons salt
½ cup unsulfured raisins
1 cup dry granola
2½ to 3 cups whole wheat flour
2 tablespoons melted butter
2 tablespoons ground cinnamon

The Glaze:

1 egg yolk
1 tablespoon water

2 tablespoons granola

In a large bowl, dissolve the yeast in the water and add the oil, honey, white flour, and salt. Beat for about 5 minutes with an electric mixer (or about 10 minutes by hand), until the mixture is quite elastic.

Mix in the raisins and granola.

Add 1 cup of the whole wheat flour and beat for about a minute with a wooden spoon. Add a second cup, and beat again (this last takes muscle).

Spread ¼ cup of whole wheat flour on your kneading board, scrape the batter onto it, sprinkle some more flour over the top, and begin to work in the flour.

Knead for about 7 minutes, adding more flour as necessary, until the dough is no longer sticky but it is still soft. (For us, that is usually an additional ¾ cup of flour.)

Pour about 1 teaspoon of oil into the scraped-out mixing bowl, put the dough in, and turn it until all sides are oiled.

Put to rise, covered with a warm wet towel, in a warm, draft-free place for about an hour, or until the dough has clearly doubled and passes the finger test (see page 6).

Grease two 8½-inch loaf pans.

Lightly flour the board again, punch the dough down, and scrape it out onto the board.

With a floured rolling pin (and turning the dough and dusting the board a few times as you roll it), roll out the dough into a rectangle roughly 14 inches by 17 inches, with square corners (see page 57).

When rolled out, brush the melted butter over the entire surface with a pastry brush and sprinkle with all the cinnamon.

Now, beginning with a narrow side, roll the dough up into a *tight* spiral. Pinch the seam a bit to close it.

Cut the roll in half, and put each half, seam side down, into a loaf pan.

To glaze the loaves: Mix the egg yolk with the water and stir until uniform, and brush onto the tops of the loaves with a pastry brush. Sprinkle about a tablespoon of granola over each loaf.

Cover the loaves with a dry towel and set to rise in a warm, draft-free place, for about ½ hour. The loaves should rise about 50 percent.

Starting in a cold oven set at 375°F., bake for 35 to 40 minutes, or until the loaves test done (see page 7).

Turn the loaves out of the pans and cool on a wire rack before serving.

Soy-Cheese
Coffee-Can Bread

This is a no-knead bread, but not a no-work bread—there is some energetic beating with a wooden spoon. However, it is a taste and nutrition winner, and it makes spectacular *round* sandwiches.

We start this bread in the blender, though a food processor would also do.

The coffee cans called for are *one-pound cans*, not the 13-ounce cans used by some coffee companies.

We use so little soy flour because soy is sticky and difficult to work with.

MAKES 2 LOAVES IN 1-POUND COFFEE CANS

1¼ cups hot water (about 125°F., see page 9)
2 tablespoons honey
1 package active dry yeast
¼ cup unsaturated oil
1¼ cups whole wheat flour

½ teaspoon salt
1 tablespoon caraway seeds
¾ cup grated cheddar cheese
1½ cups whole wheat flour (additional)
½ cup soy flour

In the container of your blender or processor combine the hot water, honey, yeast, and oil, and blend briefly.

Add the 1¼ cups of whole wheat flour and the salt, and blend slowly until well mixed, then at medium speed for about 1½ minutes. Do be sure that even the batter around the edges gets to the blades. The batter will be the texture of split-pea soup.

Pour the batter into a 2-quart or larger bowl, and set to rise, covered with a warm, wet towel, in a very warm, draft-free place for about 1 hour.

When risen, stir down.

Add ½ cup of the additional whole wheat flour, and beat with a wooden spoon for about 150 strokes (we did warn you). Repeat with the next ½ cup. Add the final ½ cup and beat for about 75 strokes. This beating develops the cohesiveness of the gluten and leaves the dough very wet.

Add the soy flour, and mix in well with the wooden spoon (no need to beat).

Put to rise, covered with a warm, wet towel, in that warm place, for about 1 hour. It should double.

Grease two 1-pound coffee cans very well.

When the dough is risen, flour your hand and punch it down, and divide it in half. Put each half in a coffee can, pressing it down into the corners.

Put the cans in a warm place, covered with a dry towel, to rise for about ½ hour, or until the cans are almost full.

Starting in a cold oven set for 375°F., bake for about 35 minutes, or until the bread tests done with a cake tester (see page 7). There will be little additional rise in the oven.

Slide a thin knife around the inside of the can, invert the can, and turn the bread out. (Tap the top of the inverted can against a hard surface if the bread resists coming out.)

Cool upright on a wire rack.

Date Corn Bread

Corn bread is easy to make, no kneading, no yeast, and no preliminary rising. (It gets all its rise in the oven from baking powder—see page 6).

The dates give this bread a marvelous flavor, but dates are often sticky and messy to chop (and prechopped dates from the market usually have sugar added). So we chop our dates in our blender with the ½ cup of flour from the recipe; the job just takes a few seconds and nothing sticks to the blades or the container!

MAKES 1 7½-INCH LOAF

1½ cups yellow cornmeal
½ cup whole wheat flour
½ cup pitted dates
½ teaspoon salt
1 tablespoon baking powder

¼ cup unsaturated oil
½ cup nonfat milk
3 tablespoons honey
2 large eggs, at room temperature

Preheat your oven to 400°F.

Measure the cornmeal into a large bowl.

Pour the whole wheat flour and dates into a blender or food processor and chop coarsely at low speed. Add to the cornmeal.

Add the salt and baking powder, and stir together until fairly uniform.

Combine the oil, milk, honey, and eggs in another bowl, and beat with a fork until smooth.

Pour the liquid ingredients over the dry ingredients and mix until fairly uniform.

Grease a 7½-inch loaf pan well and pour the the batter in.

Bake for about 35 minutes, or until the loaf is brown on top and tests done (see page 7). The batter will rise to just fill the pan.

Turn out of the pan and cool on a wire rack.

Peanut Corn Bread

This is a fun bread, easy to put together, and the peanuts make it especially attractive to children. Peanuts are really legumes, not nuts, and as such they are a good supplement for the protein in the corn.

◊ *If you do not like, or are allergic to, peanuts, use hazelnuts or walnuts (almonds are too bland).*

MAKES 1 8-INCH-SQUARE BREAD

1 cup shelled unsalted peanuts
2 cups yellow cornmeal
2 teaspoons baking soda
1 teaspoon baking powder
½ cup yogurt

⅝ cup milk (½ cup + 2 tablespoons)
2 tablespoons honey
2 large eggs, at room temperature

Preheat your oven to 400°F.

Grease well an 8- by 8-inch baking pan.

Grind the peanuts coarsely until part meal and part larger chunks. Pour into a large bowl.

Add the cornmeal, baking soda, and baking powder, and stir until fairly uniform.

Measure all the wet ingredients into a second bowl; stir until smooth, and pour over the dry ingredients.

Stir until everything is wet.

Pour the batter into the baking pan and bake for 25 minutes, or until the top is browned and the bread tests done (see page 7).

Cool in the pan, and serve warm or cool.

Southern Spoon Bread

This is called a bread, but you cannot slice it, tear it, or spread anything on it—it is just too soft to handle. Spoon bread is more of a pudding than anything else, and in the South it is traditionally served as a side dish. (That probably shows its British origins.)

Spoon bread is risen by baking soda (see page 6).

MAKES 1 8-INCH SQUARE BREAD

2 cups water	1 cup yogurt
½ teaspoon salt	3 large eggs, at room temperature
1 cup yellow cornmeal	½ teaspoon baking soda
2 tablespoons unsaturated oil	¼ cup warm water

Preheat your oven to 375°F.

Stir the cornmeal into the boiling salted water, and continue to stir for about 1 minute, until the mixture is the texture of thick oatmeal.

Remove from the heat, and allow to stand for a few minutes, to cool a little.

Mix in the oil and the yogurt, stirring until smooth. Grease an 8-inch square baking pan.

In a large bowl, beat the eggs with a whisk until pale, well risen, and very frothy. Then beat in the cornmeal mixture, until smooth.

Dissolve the baking soda in ¼ cup of warm water, and mix well (and briefly) into the rest of the ingredients.

Pour the mixture into the baking pan, and bake for about 40 minutes. There is no need to test for doneness, but all the egg should be set, not runny.

Serve hot, spooned onto the dinner plate.

Dessert Spoon Bread

Here's a variation on Southern Spoon Bread that makes it into a delicious dessert—not too sweet, but very tasty.

MAKES 1 8-INCH-SQUARE BREAD

½ cup unsulfured seedless raisins
2 cups water
½ teaspoon salt
1 cup yellow cornmeal
2 tablespoons honey

2 tablespoons unsaturated oil
1 cup yogurt
3 large eggs, at room temperature
½ teaspoon baking soda
¼ cup warm water

Preheat your oven to 375°F.

Combine the raisins, water, and salt in a saucepan and bring to a boil.

Stir in the cornmeal, and continue to stir for a minute, until the texture is like that of thick oatmeal.

Add the honey, oil, and yogurt to the cornmeal mixture and stir in well.

Grease well an 8-inch-square baking pan.

In a large bowl, beat the eggs with a whisk until very frothy and well risen. Then beat in the cornmeal mixture, until as smooth as you can make it with the raisins.

Dissolve the soda in the warm water, and mix it into the other ingredients.

Scrape the mixture into the baking pan and bake for 40 minutes. There is no need to test for doneness.

Serve hot, spooned into dessert dishes.

Corn Flatbread

Here is a marvelously delicious unleavened flatbread to have with your meals or snacks—or to take along on picnics or hikes like a cracker. The cornmeal tastes sweet, even without an added sweetener.

◊ *We use a stone-ground cornmeal which is fairly coarse.*
◊ *Do not overbrown—just the edges should be brown—or the corn will become bitter.*
◊ *Do not make these flatbreads thicker than the ¹⁄₁₆ inch called for, or they may bake up too hard to chew.*

MAKES 16 FLATBREADS

2 cups yellow cornmeal	½ teaspoon salt
2 cups water	2 tablespoons unsaturated oil

Preheat your oven to 400°F.

Lightly grease two large cookie sheets.

Measure the cornmeal into a large mixing bowl.

In a saucepan, combine the water, salt, and oil, bring to a boil, then pour over the cornmeal. Stir briskly until all the water is absorbed and the mixture is uniform.

Divide into sixteen roughly equal pieces, and roll the pieces into balls.

Flatten the balls between your fingers until about 6 inches across, more-or-less round (just squeeze together any breaks in the edges), and about ¹⁄₁₆ inch thick.

In the course of shaping, when the mixture begins to stick to your fingers, wash and dry your hands, and then continue.

Place the rounds on the cookie sheet, almost touching, eight to a sheet.

Bake for about 25 minutes until the flatbreads are just brown around the edges and crisp.

Delicious direct from the oven or cold.

~ 10 ~

Sourdough Breads—
Trapping the Wild Yeast

THE "Sourdoughs" were Alaskan prospectors. They were called Sourdoughs because while prospecting they carried around with them a bit of homemade yeast (a "sourdough starter") which had begun life as soured milk and flour, and which they had, no doubt, bought from or been given by some earlier Sourdough. They would carry this starter (mostly dry from the addition of flour) wrapped up inside their packs, or inside their shirts to keep it from freezing. When they camped, they would mix it with water and flour to make dough, saving some of this dough for a starter for the next camp.

On the West Coast and in Alaska, it is claimed that some of those original strains of sourdough starter, which may have come over with the Russian settlers of Alaska, are still alive.

What is sourdough? Actually, it's a dough in which free yeast has begun to grow. Wild yeast spores are in the air around us all the time, and if you can encourage them to grow in a favorable medium, they will multiply and act for you like commercial yeasts—with the major difference that they produce a distinctive "sour," winey, rich flavor that can really turn your tastebuds on.

If you already own some sourdough starter or know someone who'll give you some, skip the next section and go on to "Doubling the Starter," page 160.

TRAPPING THE WILD YEAST

You can buy good strains of sourdough starter in some health food stores or by mail-order (for example, from Walnut Acres, Penns Creek, Pennsylvania 17862).

We've seen recipes that describe a "sourdough" starter made with ordinary yeast and vinegar—but that's not even close.

Or you can get your sourdough starter the way we got ours—by trapping the wild yeast into a favorable medium (they love a wet, warm mixture of milk and flour).

We started with 1 cup of milk. (Even if you use whole milk for everything else, we suggest you start here with skim. The evenly distributed fat molecules of homogenized milk tend to hide the early stages of souring—when the wild yeast is getting a foothold.)

We covered the cup with a bit of cloth to keep out dust, and left it on our sideboard for almost 2 days, until it smelled sour.

Once it soured, we added 1 cup of flour, stirred the mixture, and covered it again. (Note: 1 cup milk + 1 cup flour = about 1 cup of starter.)

Within 2 days, the mixture had begun to make bubbles and had taken on a spongy look. The liquid had separated a little, but we stirred that back in. And we had the start of our starter!

If there had been no bubbles by the fifth day after putting out the milk, we would have discarded the mixture and started over.

If there had been colored molds on top, we would have discarded the mixture and started over with more milk and less flour. (Molds usually mean the mixture was too dry—molds like a drier medium than do yeasts.)

DOUBLING THE STARTER

Now we had a cup of starter. But since most sourdough recipes call for at least 1 cup, we had to "double" the starter so that we would have some left over for the next time.

Here's how we double: To 1 cup of starter we add 1 cup of milk and 1 cup of flour. We stir until the mixture is fairly uniform, then leave it loosely covered at room temperature. After a few hours, when it looks spongy, we refrigerate it.

We now have 2 cups of sourdough starter.

We could bake with this starter, but it really wants a couple of weeks storage in the refrigerator to begin to "mature." Used immediately, it will rise bread, but it will not really taste as sourdough should.

CARE AND MAINTENANCE OF THE STARTER

We keep our starter in the refrigerator, loosely covered. This starter is a live and lively yeast, and it is in the nature of yeasts to make bubbles. These bubbles will pop a plastic lid that is on tight, and they may even break a sealed bottle. So leave the lid loose.

Alternatively, you can keep your refrigerated starter in a heavy ceramic crock with a locking lid. Or you can freeze it for as much as 6 months at a time.

If you don't use your refrigerated starter often, take it out and double it once a month, then give half away (with instructions) or discard it—otherwise the starter will die in its own waste products.

Frozen starter should be thawed after 6 months and rejuvenated in the same way, and then refrozen.

GENERAL SOURDOUGH TECHNIQUE

All of our sourdough recipes give instructions on a "first day—second day" basis. Sourdough yeast is slower-acting than commercial yeast and needs about 12 hours to grow enough to rise bread.

The first day—or very early in the morning of the baking day—you put together a very *wet* mixture, which, because of its bubbly look, is known as the sponge.

The sponge is made with starter, a part of the flour, the sweetener, and all the liquid. Do not put in the salt—it will retard the yeast action slightly.

On the second day, when the sponge is risen (which means that the wild yeast has multiplied in the mixture), add the rest of the ingredients, knead, and then shape the loaves.

After shaping, you again need extra time, generally 2 to 3 hours, to rise the loaves. (Longer, if your kitchen is cold.)

◊ *Most of our sourdough recipes call for a little baking soda, to provide some extra rising help. But never use more than the amount of soda called for—any extra soda could leave an unpleasant taste. If you wish, the soda can be omitted, leaving you with a slightly lower bread and a slightly more acid flavor.*

Sourdough French Bread

The flavor of this bread is a marvel, but it won't rise quite as high as our basic French or our Quick-Rising French. Sourdough yeast just doesn't have the rising "kick" of active dry or quick-rising yeast.

◊ *To develop a good crust, we put a pan of boiling water in the oven to create steam, and we spray the loaves three times with water.*

◊ *For a more nutritious and tastier bread, substitute ½ cup of wheat germ for ½ cup of flour, in the bowl on the second day.*

◊ *Or, for Sourdough Tan French, substitute whole wheat flour for all the white flour used the second day.*

◊ *For a deeper colored crust, glaze with a mixture of egg white and 1 teaspoon of water. During the last 10 minutes of baking, brush on the glaze, then sprinkle with sesame seeds.*

MAKES 2 LOAVES

The First Day

1 cup sourdough starter
1½ cups warm water (about 110°F., see page 9)

1 tablespoon honey
3½ cups unbleached enriched white flour

The Second Day

1 tablespoon salt
½ teaspoon baking soda
2 to 3 cups unbleached enriched white flour

4 tablespoons yellow cornmeal

In a large bowl, prepare the sponge, mixing together the starter, water, honey, and 2 cups of the flour. Stir until smooth.

Add the remaining 1½ cups flour and stir until all the flour is well mixed.

Cover the bowl with waxed paper or plastic wrap and a dry towel, and set aside, out of drafts, at room temperature, for at least 12 hours.

Next day, remove the towel and the waxed paper, and stir the sponge down to its original size.

Sprinkle the salt and soda over the surface and stir in well.

Add ½ cup of the flour and stir until it disappears.

Spread 1 cup of the flour onto the kneading board, scrape the dough onto it, then spread another ½ cup over the dough, and work the flour in.

Knead in as much of the final cup of flour as required to make a soft, smooth, and very elastic dough, and then knead for about 10 minutes, until those wrinkles that signify sufficient kneading (see page 3) appear. Dust your hands lightly as required to keep the dough from sticking.

Grease two large baking sheets and sprinkle them each with 2 tablespoons of cornmeal. Tap each sheet to spread the cornmeal evenly.

Cut the dough in half, and roll each half on the board to shape a long, thin loaf, about 1½ to 2 inches thick, and long enough to stretch diagonally across your baking sheet.

Cover the loaves with a dry towel and put in a warm, draft-free place to rise for 2 to 3 hours, or until the loaves are considerably larger.

When the loaves have risen, spray the tops generously with cool water.

With a single-edged razor, or a very sharp knife, make three or four diagonal slashes equally spaced down the top of each loaf to a depth of about ⅛ inch. Do not slash too deep or the bread will fall.

Just before baking, put a pan in the bottom of the oven and pour in 2 cups of boiling water.

Starting in a cold oven, set for 375°F., bake for 30 to 35 minutes, until a golden tan.

After 5 minutes of baking, gently pull the loaves forward and spray them again. Five minutes later, spray a third time.

When the loaves test done (see page 7), remove and cool briefly on a wire rack, then serve hot, torn apart.

Sourdough Pan Loaves

This is a moister recipe than most of the sourdough breads, and it yields a lively batter. We make it in a 6-quart bowl—large enough to hold the sponge as it rises overnight, and large enough to knead in later on.

That's right, this bread uses no kneading board; it is kneaded right *in the bowl.* When you knead in the bowl, not as much flour is required to keep the dough from sticking, so the dough in the bowl winds up much moister and softer, and the bread in the pan winds up lighter.

You'll enjoy the crisp crust of this bread.

◇ *For some extra crunchy backtalk in this bread, substitute ½ cup cornmeal for ½ cup of the wheat germ.*

◇ *Or, for* Oatmeal Sourdough Bread, *substitute 1 cup of oatmeal for the wheat germ.*

MAKES 2 LARGE LOAVES IN 9½-INCH PANS

The First Day

1 cup sourdough starter	2 tablespoons honey
2½ cups warm water (about 110°F., see page 9)	5 cups unbleached enriched white flour

The Second Day

3 tablespoons unsaturated oil	1 cup wheat germ
1 tablespoon salt	1½ to 2 cups unbleached enriched white flour
1 scant teaspoon baking soda	

In a large bowl, prepare the sponge: Mix together the starter, water, and honey, and stir until smooth. Mix in the first flour.

Cover with a piece of waxed paper or plastic wrap and a dry towel, and set aside in a draft-free place to rise overnight or for about 12 hours at room temperature.

The next day, stir the sponge down, add the oil, salt, and baking soda, and mix until blended. Add the wheat germ and mix in.

Add 1½ cups of the flour, ½ cup at a time, beating and then kneading each in well before adding the next ½ cup. Add no more flour, except what is needed to keep your hands from sticking as you knead in the bowl.

Knead in the bowl for about 10 minutes. This dough will not fully stop sticking to your hands, but it is ready when the dough ball shows cohesion when you pick it up and let it hang from your hand.

If you're not sure, knead some more.

Grease two 9½ by 5½-inch loaf pans.

Divide the dough in half, form each half into a loaf shape, put into the pans, and with your fingers even off the loaves so that they are fairly level.

Cover the loaves with a dry towel and set to rise in a warm, draft-free place for 1½ to 2 hours, until the dough rises to almost fill the pans.

Starting in a cold oven set for 375°F., bake for about 45 minutes, until the loaves test done (see page 7).

Turn out onto a wire rack and let cool for several minutes before slicing.

Sourdough English Muffins

You don't get English muffins in England—there you have to ask for "scones" (which rhymes with "on").

This bread is cooked not in an oven but on a griddle. The directions call for the griddle to be set at low heat, and when we say low, we mean simmering low. It will take an extra 5 minutes for the griddle to preheat at low, but once it's heated, the muffins cook up in only 4 to 5 minutes per side. This gives you a muffin that is moist but cooked through. A higher temperature can give you a muffin that is almost scorched outside but still uncooked at its center. Like all sourdough breads, this has to be started the day before, so try to get that "I-want-English-Muffins-for-breakfast" feeling before you go to bed.

◊ *If you are cooking for kids, substitute whole milk for skim.*

◊ *You can substitute ½ cup of wheat germ for ½ cup of white flour in the sponge.*

◊ *Or, substitute whole wheat flour for all of the flour used the next morning.*

◊ *When you roll out the dough, do try to get it to a ½-inch thickness. Thicker, and the muffins may not get cooked; thinner, and they don't have that satisfying bulk.*

◊ *The cornmeal sprinkled on the wax paper and over the rising muffins serves to keep the raw muffins from sticking to each other, the paper, and the griddle. It also gives a delightful crunch to the crusts.*

◊ *This recipe yields 30 English muffins, with a 3-inch round cutter. If that is too many, reserve half or two thirds of the kneaded dough in your refrigerator for as long as a week (see page 232), then allow the dough to come to room temperature before working it. Or cook all the muffins and freeze as many as you wish for future toasting.*

◊ *If you wish to, use a square cutter or an oblong cutter—or any shape. But the muffins may not rise as high as the circles.*

◊ *For* Sourdough Sandwich Bread, *divide the kneaded dough in half; put into two well-greased 8-inch loaf pans; rise, warm, for about an hour; then bake at 350°F. for about 40 minutes, or until the loaves test done (see page 7).*

MAKES ABOUT 30 MUFFINS

The Night Before

1 cup sourdough starter	4 cups unbleached enriched white
2 tablespoons honey	flour
2 cups warm nonfat milk (about 110°F., see page 9)	

The Next Morning

1 scant teaspoon baking soda	¼ cup cornmeal
2 teaspoons salt	
1 to 2 cups unbleached enriched white flour	

In a large bowl, prepare the sponge: Mix together the starter, honey, and milk, and stir briefly.

Add the flour, 2 cups at a time, and mix until thoroughly wet.

Cover with a piece of plastic wrap or waxed paper and a dry towel, and leave at room temperature to rise overnight in a draft-free place.

About 12 hours later, uncover the sponge mixture and stir it down.

Sprinkle the baking soda and salt over the sponge and mix in thoroughly.

Sprinkle 1 cup of the flour over the kneading board and scrape the batter over it.

Knead in this cup, and as much more of another cup as required to make a dough that is medium-stiff and does not stick to your hands. When the dough stops sticking, knead for another 5 minutes, dusting your hands lightly if necessary.

Spread waxed paper on a couple of large baking sheets, and sprinkle with cornmeal.

Flour the kneading board lightly and roll out the dough to about ½ inch thick. With a 3-inch round cutter, cut as many rounds as you can from your rolled-out dough.

As cut, place the rounds on the cornmealed waxed paper, leaving room so that they do not touch and stick together.

When you've cut all the rounds possible, knead the leftover dough together, and roll out again, and cut again, until you've shaped all the dough.

Sprinkle the tops of the shaped muffins with a little more cornmeal.

Cover with a dry towel and set in a warm, draft-free place to rise for ½ hour, or until the muffins are about ¾ inch high.

When risen, butter your griddle and preheat it to a low temperature—until a drop of water skitters over the surface.

Use a pancake turner to remove the muffins from the paper and transport them to the griddle, four to a batch. Don't allow them to touch.

Cook on each side for 4 to 5 minutes. If they begin to rise in the middle, gently flatten just a bit with your pancake turner when you turn them onto the second side.

Open the first one and check the inside for doneness before removing the others, and taste. (Remember, this is a fresh-baked English muffin, and not toasted, as you are used to them.)

If desired, split and toast them right away.

Sour Pumpernickel

Robust is the word that best describes Sour Pumpernickel. Pile on the strong cheese and the onions and mustard—this bread still keeps its character and flavor. The texture of the loaf is medium-light—just right for a sandwich, and excellent for toasting as well.

The overnight rise makes this pumpernickel easier to knead than most rye recipes.

◊ *We spray the loaves with water to develop a good, thick crust.*
◊ *Rye flour can make for a heavy bread, so don't force in more of the white flour than required to handle the dough.*
◊ *If you don't want the shininess or the caraway seeds of the glaze, skip that step.*

MAKES 3 LOAVES

The First Day

1 cup sourdough starter
2 cups nonfat milk
2 tablespoons blackstrap molasses
¼ cup unsaturated oil

1 cup unbleached white flour
1 cup whole rye flour
2 cups whole wheat flour

The Second Day

1 tablespoon salt
scant ½ teaspoon baking soda
½ cup whole rye flour
1 to 1½ cups unbleached enriched
    white flour

1 tablespoon caraway seeds
¼ cup white cornmeal

The Glaze (optional):

egg yolk
1 tablespoon water

1 tablespoon caraway seeds

Make up the sponge by combining in a large bowl all the first-day ingredients, mixing in the flour 1 cup at a time until the mixture is wet and smooth.

Cover with a wet towel and allow to stand overnight in a draft-free place.

At least 12 hours later, stir the sponge down to its original size. Sprinkle the salt and soda over the surface and stir in.

Stir in the rye flour.

Pour 1 cup of the white flour over your kneading board, scrape the batter onto it, and knead the flour in. Then knead in the caraway seeds.

This dough never completely stops sticking, so you can expect to use another ½ cup of white flour to sprinkle the board and your hands as you knead for another 5 minutes to achieve a dough that can just be handled.

Grease two baking sheets and sprinkle them with white cornmeal. Tap the sheets to spread the cornmeal evenly.

Divide the dough into thirds and shape into three oblong loaves. Place two loaves on one sheet and one loaf on the other, leaving room between the two loaves for spread.

With a sharp knife or a single-edged razor, slash each loaf diagonally with three slashes, ¼ to ½ inch deep.

Cover the loaves with a dry towel and put into a warm, draft-free place to rise for 2 to 3 hours. The loaves will look well risen and the slashes will gape wide.

Gently, slash again into the same slashes, but only ⅛ inch deep. Spray the loaves with water.

Starting in a cold oven set for 375°F., bake for 40 minutes.

After the loaves have been in the oven for 10 minutes, pull forward and spray them again.

After 30 minutes, apply the glaze: Mix the egg yolk and water together, brush thinly over the loaves with a pastry brush, then quickly sprinkle with caraway seeds.

After 40 minutes, when the loaves *almost* pass a test for doneness (see page 7), shut off the oven and allow to sit in the closed oven for another 10 minutes. This avoids scorching.

Cool on a wire rack and serve warm.

Sour Rye

"Sour Rye" is what it says when you buy this style of bread packaged, or it may be known as "Jewish Rye" or even "New York Rye."

One reason that some commercial rye breads seem so light and fluffy compared to home-baked ryes (aside from their being machine kneaded and aerated) is that most commercial bakers use very little rye flour, substituting caramel coloring to get the dark look of rye.

◊ *Rye flour can make a heavy bread, so don't force in more of the white flour than required to make a dough that can be handled.*

◊ *This recipe calls for 2 cups of milk but you can use plain water or fruit juice, or chicken soup, or beer—any liquid. The liquid makes only a small difference in the end flavor, but that small difference can be the difference between "good" and "special." We often use soup stock.*

◊ *For a shiny loaf, glaze with a thin smearing of egg yolk and water at about 30 minutes of baking, as described for Sour Pumpernickel (page 170). If you glaze, you can add a sprinkling of caraway seeds.*

◊ *For a thicker crust, spray with tepid water before the loaves go into the oven and after they have been baking for 10 minutes.*

◊ *For a little interest, add 1 tablespoon of caraway seeds, dill seeds, Russian caraway, or sesame seeds to the batter on the second day.*

MAKES 3 LOAVES

The First Day

1 cup sourdough starter
2 cups nonfat milk
¼ cup unsaturated oil
2 tablespoons blackstrap molasses

2 cups whole rye flour
2 cups unbleached enriched white flour

The Second Day

1 tablespoon salt
scant ½ teaspoon baking soda
1 cup whole rye flour

2 to 2½ cups unbleached enriched
    white flour
¼ cup white cornmeal

In a large mixing bowl, prepare the sponge by combining all the first-day ingredients and mixing until smooth.

Cover with a wet, warm towel and put into a draft-free place to rise for about 12 hours or overnight.

The next day, stir down the sponge, sprinkle the salt and soda over it, and mix in well.

Add the rye flour, and stir in until all wet.

Pour 1 cup of the white flour over the kneading board, dump the batter onto it, and work in the flour.

Add another cup of white flour, and knead it in.

Sprinkle flour on the board, and knead for about 10 minutes, working in only as much of the remaining flour as required to make this dough manageable. When ready, the dough will feel springy, and you will see the wrinkles that are characteristic of sufficient kneading on its surface (see page 3).

Grease two baking sheets and sprinkle each with about 2 tablespoons of cornmeal.

Divide the dough into three equal parts and shape into oblong loaves. Place two loaves on one sheet, leaving room for spread, and one loaf on the other.

Slash the loaves diagonally with a sharp knife or single-edged razor, three or four slashes per loaf, cover with a dry towel, and put into a warm place to rise for 2 to 3 hours. The slashes will gape wide when the loaf is ready.

Starting in a cold oven set at 375°F., bake for about 40 minutes. If a test for doneness (see page 7) shows the loaves to be *almost* done, shut off the flame and allow the loaves to sit in the oven for another 10 minutes.

Cool on a wire rack and serve fairly cool.

Snack Bread

If you are looking for a chewy, strong-flavored sourdough bread that's great with cheese or salami or tongue or liverwurst or hors d'oeuvres—you've arrived.

This is a backward bread. Instead of working for lightness and rise and good texture, as with almost every other bread, here we are looking for a solid toughness that would mark failure in any other recipe.

◊ *You can use various kinds of seeds in Snack Bread: caraway, dill, fennel, Russian caraway, poppy, celery. Our favorite is the burnt flavor of Russian caraway—and we use plenty.*

◊ *These loaves rise for only ½ hour—and show little expansion. That's deliberate.*

MAKES 4 THIN LOAVES

The First Day

1 cup sourdough starter	2 tablespoons honey
1¾ cups warm water (about 110°F., see page 9)	4 cups whole wheat flour

The Second Day

2 tablespoons salt	1 cup whole rye flour
2 tablespoons seeds (your choice)	

In a large bowl, prepare the sponge: Combine the starter, water, and honey, and stir until the honey is dissolved.

Stir in the whole wheat flour until mixed and smooth.

Cover the bowl with waxed paper or plastic and a towel and set to rise in a draft-free place overnight (8 to 9 hours).

The next day, stir down the sponge, and stir in the salt and seeds.

Spread the rye flour over the board, scrape the sponge onto it, and knead in the rye flour. If more flour is required to make the dough stop sticking to the board, sprinkle on whole wheat, not rye. When the loaves stop sticking, you have kneaded enough.

Grease two large baking sheets.

Divide the dough into four roughly equal pieces. Flour the board lightly with whole wheat flour and, starting in the middle, roll each piece out to a single strand about 1 inch thick.

As each strand is rolled, place it on a baking sheet, two loaves per sheet.

Cover the loaves with dry towels, and put into a warm place to rise for ½ to ¾ hour. There will be little rise (if there is none, allow to rise for another 15 minutes).

Starting in a cold oven set at 375°F., bake for 30 to 40 minutes, or until the loaves test done (see page 7).

Cool on a wire rack; to serve, slice thin with a serrated knife.

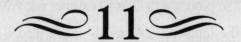

Batter Breads

BATTER is a dough that is too wet to be kneaded. With any batter bread, you could add about 25 percent more flour and be able to knead it.

Just what is the point, then, of batter breads?

Well, these moist and delicious batters give you a coarse texture quite different from other kneaded breads; they are able to carry many heavy—and tasty—ingredients that would make a kneaded bread too dense; and, while they do require plenty of mixing (some or all of which may be done in a machine), they require *no kneading*.

BATTER BREAD TECHNIQUE

All batter breads start out the same way. The liquids are combined with part of the flour and this mixture is beaten to develop elasticity. Most of the beating is done early, before all the flour has been added, when the batter is still thin and easy to work. Begin beating with a whisk, but as the batter gets stiffer you'll need a wooden spoon.

The rest of the flour is then beaten in, a bit at a time, until the beating becomes too difficult. Then the last of the flour is worked in with a bare hand: The batter is squeezed between the fingers.

There is personal satisfaction to be had in beating one of these breads from beginning to end by hand. If that is your preference, do it.

176

But no one comes around giving medals to those who beat batter breads entirely by hand. A food processor can beat these breads all the way through, and there is no noticeable difference in the finished batter bread. The processor will cut the work time by two thirds. But we prefer that the last bit of flour be worked in by hand. Beat in the processor until the batter shows a lot of cohesion, then scrape it out into a bowl and get the last of the flour in by squeezing the batter between your fingers.

A blender can do a lot of the work, but it will labor as the batter gets really cohesive, as it must. If you do not mind making the machine labor, use the blender until the batter shows itself to be very elastic, and then scrape out, and work in the last of the flour by squeezing between your fingers. The blender will also cut mixing time by two thirds.

Any electric mixer can manage the early stages of beating the batter, and larger models can get you quite a way through. But you will find that the more elastic the batter becomes, the more tendency it shows to climb up the beaters and attack the machine. An electric beater cuts mixing time in half.

The batter is messy and the scraping out of the batter and the subsequent cleaning of the processor, the blender, or the beaters is frustrating and time-consuming.

Beating times are variable. Fastest by machine, of course, slowest if you can't hand-beat vigorously. By hand or by machine, the batter must be beaten until it is *very* elastic.

When the batter is beaten, it is set to rise, just as with a kneaded dough. When risen, the batter will be a little easier to handle, though still sticky.

Grease (not flour) your hand lightly, punch down the batter, and *press* out (not knead out) the larger bubbles.

The batter is then put into a well-greased container for baking: casserole, baking pan, soufflé dish, etc. Fill the container *no more than halfway* or the loaf may sag.

Once the batter is in the container, grease a spatula (or your hand) and poke it into the corners and smooth it out as best you can. Imperfections left on the surface stay there through the baking.

◊ *Don't skimp on the first rise, but don't let the second rise go beyond the lip of the container or the bread may collapse. (If it collapses, knead down and put to rise again. Nothing lost but time.)*

◊ *Leftover batter spooned into greased muffin pans makes won-derful drop rolls that bake in 20 to 25 minutes (see page 236). Fill the containers less than half full.*

◊ *Here's a hint: When you change from whisk to spoon (or beaters) to fingers, clean the batter off the implement—or your fingers— by dipping into a separate container of flour and then rubbing the batter off into the mixing bowl.*

Cottage Casserole

This is our favorite batter bread. The seeds and onion give it an eye-popping flavor, while the cottage cheese makes for a unique texture and also makes it high in protein. Just add a salad and you have a complete meal.

We bake this bread in a casserole, which gives it a crust so crisp and tasty it is hard to imagine this a bread rather than some exotic fried dish.

◊ *If you want to substitute pot cheese or farmer cheese (which are drier than cottage cheese), add ¼ cup warm nonfat milk.*

◊ *For variety, try caraway, fennel, anise, or celery seeds.*

◊ *For a touch of adventure, substitute dry minced garlic for the onion.*

◊ *Bran can be substituted for all or part of the wheat germ.*

MAKES 1 LARGE LOAF IN A 1½-QUART CASSEROLE

1½ cups cottage cheese	1 tablespoon dill seed
1 tablespoon unsaturated oil	1 teaspoon salt
1½ packages active dry yeast	1 large egg, at room temperature
2 tablespoons honey	2 cups unbleached enriched white
1 tablespoon dry minced onion (or onion flakes)	flour
	¼ cup wheat germ

In a small saucepan combine the cottage cheese and oil, and heat to about 140°F.—quite warm but not hot enough to burn.

In a large bowl, combine the cottage cheese with the yeast and stir.

Add the honey, onion, dill seed, salt, and egg, and stir until well mixed.

Beat in 1 cup of the flour for 5 minutes (2 minutes by machine), beat in the wheat germ for 1 minute, and ½ cup of flour for 1 minute.

Add the final ½ cup of flour (use part of it to clean your spoon into the bowl), and squeeze between your fingers as vigorously as you can for about 2 minutes. The batter should be very cohesive.

Clean the batter off your hand into the bowl, cover the bowl with a clean towel, and put to rise in a warm, draft-free place until doubled—less than 1 hour.

Generously grease a 1½ quart casserole.

When risen, punch the batter down and gently press out the larger air bubbles.

Scrape the batter into the casserole, press it into the corners, and smooth the top. The batter should fill it halfway.

Cover again, and put to rise again for about half the time of the first rise—or *until the dough comes just to the lip of the casserole*.

Starting in a cold oven set for 350°F., bake for 35 to 40 minutes, or until the bread is brown on top and tests done (see page 7).

Turn out of the casserole and bring right to the table.

Anadama Bread

This adaptation of a very old American recipe makes a handsome loaf that is delicious, crunchy, and nutritious.

◇ *Use 100 percent whole stone-ground cornmeal; it's so much better than the degerminated pap.*
◇ *For more flavor, substitute millet meal for cornmeal.*
◇ *For a sweeter loaf, substitute honey for molasses.*
◇ *If you do not wish to glaze with butter, brush on milk instead, and then sprinkle on the cornmeal. If you've used millet meal, substitute that in the glazing.*
◇ *For extra crunch, sprinkle the buttered pan with cornmeal before the batter goes in.*

MAKES 1 LARGE LOAF IN A 9-INCH PAN

The Batter:

1 package active dry yeast
1 cup hot skim milk (about 125°F., see page 9)
3 tablespoons unsaturated oil
3 tablespoons blackstrap molasses
1½ teaspoons salt

3½ cups unbleached enriched white flour
2 large eggs, at room temperature
¼ cup wheat germ
½ cup whole yellow cornmeal

The Glaze:

melted butter   1 tablespoon cornmeal

In a large bowl, combine the yeast and milk, and stir.

Stir in the oil, molasses, and salt.

Add the first 2 cups of flour and beat by hand for 5 minutes (2 by machine).

Beat in the eggs for 1 minute each, then the wheat germ for 1 minute, the cornmeal for 1 minute, and 1 cup of flour for 2 minutes.

Clean your spoon (or beaters) into the batter (see page 11), add the final ½ cup of flour, and work with your bare hand for 2 to 3 minutes, as vigorously as you can. The batter must be quite elastic.

Scrape the batter from your hand into the bowl, cover the bowl with a dry towel, and set to rise in a warm, draft-free place for about 1¼ hours, or until doubled.

When risen, grease your hand and punch the dough down, then press it to get rid of the larger bubbles.

Grease well a 9 by 5½-inch loaf pan.

Scrape the batter in, then press it into the corners and smooth out the top.

To glaze the loaf: Brush melted butter over the top with a pastry brush, then sprinkle with cornmeal.

Cover and put to rise again, until the batter reaches the lip of the pan—about half the time of the first rise.

Starting in a cold oven set for 375°F., bake for 35 to 40 minutes, until the top is dark brown and the loaf tests done (see page 7).

Turn out of the pan, cool briefly on a wire rack, and serve hot.

Light Rye Batter Bread

The flavor of rye flour complements the coarse texture of a batter bread, but it makes for the stickiest of batters.

◇ *Russian caraway can be substituted for the caraway seeds.*

◇ *Wheat germ can be substituted for ½ cup of rye flour.*

◇ *For a glaze, brush on melted butter with a pastry brush just before the final rise, and sprinkle with additional caraway seeds.*

◇ *Do not fill the casserole more than halfway—any extra batter makes excellent drop rolls. To make Light Rye Batter Drop Rolls, drop ¼-cup lumps of batter onto a greased baking sheet or greased muffin pan. Allow to rise for 15 minutes. Starting in a cold oven set for 375°F., bake for 20 to 25 minutes.*

MAKES 1 LARGE LOAF IN A 2-QUART CASSEROLE

2 packages active dry yeast
2 tablespoons caraway seeds
2 teaspoons salt
¼ cup unsaturated oil
¼ cup honey

1½ cups hot nonfat skim milk (about 125°F., see page 9)
2 cups unbleached enriched white flour
2 cups whole rye flour

Into a large bowl measure the yeast, seeds, salt, oil, honey, and milk. Stir well.

Mix in the white flour, 1 cup at a time, beating well between cups, and then continue beating for about 5 minutes by hand (about 2 minutes by machine).

Beat in 1 cup of the rye flour for 2 minutes.

Clean off your spoon or beaters (see page 11). Add the last cup of rye flour, and work with your hand for 3 minutes, squeezing the batter between your fingers.

Scrape the batter off your hand into the bowl, cover with a hot, *wet* towel, and set to rise in a warm, draft-free place until doubled—about 1½ hours.

When risen, punch down and press out the larger air bubbles.

Grease a 2-quart casserole very well. Scrape in the batter, poking and pushing it into the corners, and smoothing out the surface.

Set to rise again, covered with a clean, *dry* towel, until the batter reaches the lip of the casserole—about half the time of the first rise.

Starting in a cold oven set for 375°F., bake for 45 to 55 minutes, until the loaf tests done (see page 7).

Turn out of the casserole carefully, cool for a while on a wire rack, and serve hot.

Dark Rye Batter Bread

This is a variation of Light Rye Batter Bread for those of you with a tooth for a little stronger flavor.

◊ *Any of the variations suggested for Light Rye Batter Bread can be used here.*

MAKES 1 LARGE LOAF IN A 2½-QUART CASSEROLE

2 packages active dry yeast
2 tablespoons Russian caraway seeds
2 teaspoons salt
¼ cup unsaturated oil
¼ cup blackstrap molasses
2 cups hot skim milk (about 125°F., see page 9)

2½ cups unbleached enriched white flour
½ cup wheat germ
2¼ cups whole rye flour

Proceed as for Light Rye Batter Bread (page 182), but use a 2½-quart casserole.

SPEEDY BATTER BREADS

Speedy batter breads are batter breads, of our own invention, that are *given no first rise.* Once the batter is beaten—with the same vigorous mixing techniques as regular batter breads—they are put directly into greased baking pans. These pans are put to rise for 20 minutes, and then baked (starting in a cold oven).

These speedy batter breads will save you at least an hour of rising time.

⬦ *Be sure you follow the beating directions in the recipes to develop the elastic gluten well.*
⬦ *Fill your baking pans less than half full.*
⬦ *Never preheat your oven for these breads—they need the extra chance to rise before the yeast is killed.*
⬦ *For Speedy Batter Drop Rolls, use any of these recipes, but drop the batter into greased muffin pans (or any small molds), filling less than half full. Bake for about 25 minutes at 325°F., starting cold.*

Speedy Batter Herb Bread

The web of this bread has a satisfyingly coarse, homemade look, and the texture is unlike anything to come out of a bakery.

⬦ *To improve the bread's keeping power, add 2 tablespoons of unsaturated oil.*
⬦ *Bran or wheat germ can be substituted for ¼ cup of white flour.*
⬦ *Juggle the herbs to suit your own taste.*
⬦ *For a very attractive plain* White Speedy Batter Bread, *omit the herbs.*
⬦ *For a delicious* Tan Speedy Bread, *substitute about 50 percent*

whole wheat flour. (Tan Speedy Bread *must be beaten a little longer at each stage.*)

◊ For Pepper Herb Bread, *add ½ teaspoon of fresh-ground black pepper.*

◊ *This bread slices quite thin when cool, which makes it an excellent sandwich loaf. Or tear it apart when hot.*

MAKES 2 LOAVES IN 8½-INCH PANS

2 packages active dry yeast	2 tablespoons honey
1 teaspoon dill seed	2 cups hot nonfat milk (about
1 teaspoon savory	125°F., see page 9)
½ teaspoon dry dill weed	4½ cups unbleached enriched white
2 teaspoons salt	flour

In a large bowl combine the yeast, herbs, salt, honey, and milk, and stir well.

One cup at a time, add the first 3 cups of flour, beating each cup in well, then beat the resulting batter vigorously by hand for about 3 minutes (or by machine for 2 minutes).

Add the next cup of flour, ½ cup at a time, and beat for a minute or two for each addition. When the batter gets too stiff to beat, work it with your hand, squeezing it between your fingers.

Work in the last ½ cup of flour well. The batter is ready when it forms rubbery sheets as you pull your spoon or hand out.

Grease well two 8½-inch loaf pans.

Scrape half the batter into each pan. Grease a spatula (or your hand) and poke the batter into the corners of the pan, then smooth out the surfaces somewhat.

Cover the pans with a dry towel and set to rise in a very warm, draft-free place, for 20 minutes.

Starting in a cold oven set at 250°F., bake for 10 minutes, then raise the temperature to 375°F. and bake for an additional 40 minutes (50 minutes total), or until the loaf tests done (see page 7).

Turn out of the pans and cool on a wire rack.

Peanut Speedy Batter Bread

This may be the world's fastest yeast bread. The last loaf we baked took just *one hour and five minutes* from start to finish, not including the time it took to shell the nuts.

Because of the peanuts (and the cylindrical shape), this tan bread makes an excellent bread for children. It has a fine and even web, so honey won't drip through.

◊ *For a more sophisticated flavor, substitute filberts (hazelnuts) for the peanuts.*

◊ *For a less sophisticated flavor, add another ¼ cup of peanuts, chopped rather than ground coarsely.*

◊ *If you have no 1-pound coffee cans available, substitute a 1½-quart casserole, fill less than halfway, and make* Peanut Batter Drop Rolls *with the leftover batter (see page 236). Bake the casserole at 375°F. for 45 to 50 minutes.*

MAKES 2 LOAVES IN 1-POUND COFFEE CANS

2 packages active dry yeast
¼ cup honey
1 teaspoon salt
1¼ cup hot water (about 125°F., see page 9)

½ cup coarsely ground shelled peanuts
1½ cups whole wheat flour
1½ cups unbleached enriched white flour

In a large bowl, combine the yeast, honey, salt, and water, and stir well.

Stir in the peanuts.

Beat in 1 cup of the white flour for about 1 minute.

Add 1 cup of the whole wheat flour, stir in well, and beat vigorously for 2 minutes (1 minute by machine).

Beat in the last ½ cup of white flour for 1 minute.

Add the last ½ cup of whole wheat flour and work in by hand, squeezing the batter between your fingers. Once the flour is all wet, continue working for about 2 minutes more, until the elasticity of the batter is very well developed. Clean your hand into the bowl (see page 11).

Grease two 1-pound (not 13-ounce) coffee cans generously, then scrape half the batter into each can.

Cover the cans with a towel and set to rise in a warm, draft-free place for 20 minutes.

Starting in a cold oven set at 375°F., bake for 30 to 35 minutes, or until the tops are brown and the loaves test done (see page 7).

Turn out of the pans and cool upright on a wire rack, or serve hot.

Speedy Dark
Whole Wheat Raisin Bread

This bread is very rich in essential vitamins and minerals, and contains the complete protein and the complex carbohydrates.

◊ *We rise it in hot water (see page 5). (Whole wheat dough is slower to rise and the extra heat helps it along.)*
◊ *If you are baking for children, you can raise the butterfat level of this nutritious bread by substituting hot whole milk for the nonfat milk.*
◊ *For a shinier look, glaze with a brushing of melted butter as soon as the bread comes out of the oven.*

MAKES 2 LOAVES IN 8½-INCH PANS

2 packages active dry yeast
¼ cup blackstrap molasses
2 teaspoons salt
2 cups hot nonfat milk (about 125°F., see page 9)

2 tablespoons unsaturated oil
2 large eggs, at room temperature
4½ cups whole wheat flour
1 cup unsulfured raisins

Into a large bowl, measure the yeast, molasses, salt, and milk, and mix well.

Mix in the oil.

Break the eggs into the bowl and beat with a whisk until smooth.

Add 2 cups of the flour, 1 cup at a time, beating each cup for a minute.

Stir in another cup of flour, and beat briskly for 3 minutes by hand (or 2 minutes by machine).

Stir the raisins in well, mixing thoroughly.

Add the last 1½ cups of flour, ½ cup at a time, beating or working with your bare hand for a minute for each addition.

Grease two 8½-inch loaf pans, and spoon half the batter into each pan, filling no more than halfway.

With a buttered spatula, poke the batter into the corners of the pans, then smooth the tops of the loaves as well as you can.

Rise these pans of batter, covered with a warm, wet towel, in hot water for 20 minutes.

Starting in a cold oven set for 200°F., bake for 10 minutes; then raise the temperature to 375°F. and bake for an additional 25 to 30 minutes. Test for doneness (see page 7).

Turn the loaves out onto a wire rack and cool.

Speedy Batter Cheese Bread

This is the speedy batter bread that began it all—the first one we ever made. It's a delicious beginning. A casserole loaf of this bread has a delightfully crispy bottom and sides.

◊ *This batter stays thin enough to use a whisk throughout. But do be certain that the batter is beaten enough to be quite elastic.*

◊ *Use sharp cheddar cheese to your taste, or try another cheese altogether. Keep cold until you are ready to use it (warm cheese won't grate).*

◊ *Taste the cheese: If it is salty, reduce the recipe salt to 1 teaspoon.*

◊ *For Speedy Batter Tan Cheese Bread, use 2 cups of whole wheat flour and 2½ cups of unbleached white flour.*

◊ *Or wheat germ can be substituted for ½ cup of flour.*

◊ *You can substitute two small loaf pans for the coffee cans.*

MAKES 1 LARGE LOAF IN A 1½-QUART CASSEROLE,
PLUS 2 SMALL LOAVES IN 1-POUND COFFEE CANS

2 packages active dry yeast
3 tablespoons honey
2 teaspoons salt
2 cups hot skim milk (about 125°F., see page 9)
2 tablespoons unsaturated oil

2 cups unbleached enriched white flour
1 large egg, at room temperature
2 cups grated cheddar cheese
3 cups unbleached enriched white flour (additional)

Measure the yeast, honey, salt, and milk into a large bowl and stir well.

Stir in the oil.

Beat in the 2 cups of flour, 1 cup at a time, beating 1 minute for each cup.

Beat in the egg for 1 minute, then the cheese for 1 minute.

Add 1½ cups of the additional flour, ½ cup at a time, beating for 1 minute for each ½ cup.

Add the last 1½ cups of flour, ½ cup at a time, working each ½ cup in well.

Grease well a 1½-quart casserole and two 1-pound (not 13-ounce) coffee cans. Spoon the batter in, filling no more than halfway.

Set in a very warm place to rise, covered with a towel, for 20 minutes.

Starting in a cold oven set for 350°F., bake the coffee cans about 30 minutes, the casserole about 40 minutes. When the tops are golden brown, test for doneness (see page 7).

Turn out onto a wire rack and cool, or bring to the table hot and tear apart.

Speedy Sally Lunn

Sally Lunn was an Englishwoman who is supposed to have sold these "cakes" on the streets of Bath sometime around the end of the eighteenth century.

This bread is very like a European coffee cake: light and spongy, yellow in color, and with a distinctive flavor. It can be eaten plain or toasted, served with preserves or honey, or iced like a cake.

◊ *The juice and grated zest of a whole lemon can be substituted for the orange.*

◊ *To turn this into* Speedy Holiday Bread, *add 4 ounces of chopped dried fruits to the batter after the flour is all in.*

◊ *For* Speedy Dressy Bread, *add ¼ cup mixed chopped dates and raisins. With this combination, put the glaze on before putting the bread into the oven.*

◊ *About ¼ cup of chopped nuts can be added to either* Holiday *or* Dressy Bread.

◊ *To simplify things for yourself, drop out the glaze.*

MAKES 2 LOAVES IN 8½-INCH PANS,
OR 3 SHALLOW 9-INCH RING MOLDS

The Batter:

2 packages active dry yeast
1 teaspoon salt
⅓ cup honey
1 cup hot nonfat milk (about 125°F., see page 9)
½ cup unsaturated oil

2 cups unbleached enriched white flour
3 large eggs, at room temperature
2 cups unbleached enriched white flour (additional)

The Glaze (optional):

1 tablespoon honey
juice of ½ orange

grated zest of ½ orange

Measure the yeast, salt, honey, hot water, and milk powder into a large bowl, and stir well.

Mix in the oil, then the 2 cups of flour.

Break in the eggs, one at a time, beating each in for about 1 minute.

Add 1½ cups of the additional flour, ½ cup at a time, beating for a minute after each ½ cup.

Add the last ½ cup of flour, and work it in well with a wooden spoon. The batter should be *very elastic*. If not, beat for 2 to 3 more minutes.

Grease two 8½-inch loaf pans or three shallow 9-inch ring molds.

With a greased spoon, spoon the batter into the pans, filling less than half full. (Regrease the spoon as you work if necessary.) With a greased spoon or spatula, poke the batter into the corners and level off the surface.

Cover with a towel and set to rise in a warm, draft-free place for 20 minutes.

Starting in a cold oven set for 350°F., bake the loaf pans for about 45 minutes, the ring molds for about 30 minutes.

Meanwhile, prepare the glaze. In a small bowl, combine the honey, orange juice, and grated zest.

When Sally has baked for about 15 minutes, pull the racks forward and gently spoon the glaze over the loaves. Push the racks back in and continue baking.

When done—test with a toothpick (see page 7)—allow to cool in the pans for a few minutes, then turn out carefully onto a wire rack. Serve at least one loaf while it is hot.

∽ 12 ∽

Popovers, Croissants, and Bagels

THESE three "breads" have one thing in common; the reaction they elicit when you bring them to the table.

POPOVERS

Bread making can very inexact. You have a lot of leeway—a wide range of flours, temperatures, time, etc., will still give you successful bread. But popover making needs to be *very exact*.

Temperatures (of oven and ingredients), proportions, timing, all should be followed as exactly as you can—unless you find that your oven varies from ours. If it does, *make notes* about your experiences right on the recipes so you will have them the next time.

We "backtime" popovers: We will want to sit down to them at, say, 8:00 A.M., so we take the ingredients out of the refrigerator first thing in the morning, start the oven to preheat at 7:00 A.M., start mixing at 7:15, put in at 7:20, take out at 7:58. The rest of our life is not that organized.

◊ *Remember, all the ingredients for popovers should be at room temperature when you start.*

◊ *Popover pans are available from cookware specialists. But we use baba cups—small, tapered, heavy-gauge aluminum cups* usually used for baking individual babas-au-rhum. They hold exactly ¾ cup of fluid each and measure 3⅛ inches tall, 1¾ inches across the bottom, and 2⅜ inches across the inside measurement of the top. Grease them quite well.

◊ It is the egg and the high baking temperature that give you your rise. You will get less rise in popover recipes with the added ingredients than with the Basic Popovers.

◊ Popovers should come out crisp but not scorched. If they are not cooked well enough, they will collapse; if overcooked, they will be rigid, they may stick to the cups, and they will taste burnt.

◊ For twice as many popovers, simply double the ingredients.

Basic Popovers

MAKES 6 POPOVERS

2 large eggs, at room temperature 1 cup tepid nonfat milk 2 tablespoons unsaturated oil

1 cup unbleached enriched white flour ¼ teaspoon salt

Preheat your oven to 425°F.

Grease six ¾-cup popover cups quite well.

In a large bowl, beat the eggs lightly, then add the milk and oil and beat together briefly with a whisk.

Add the flour and salt, and beat briskly for 2 minutes with the whisk. The batter will have the consistency of thin pancake batter.

Divide the batter among the cups (filling each between half and two thirds full), and bake for 38 minutes. You should get almost triple rising.

Turn out and serve hot from the oven.

Wheat Germ Popovers

MAKES 6 POPOVERS

2 large eggs, at room temperature
1 cup tepid nonfat milk
2 tablespoons unsaturated oil

⅞ unbleached enriched white flour
2 tablespoons wheat germ
¼ teaspoon salt

Preheat your oven to 425°F.

Grease quite well six ¾-cup popover cups.

In a large bowl, beat the eggs lightly with a whisk, then beat in the milk and oil briefly.

Add the remaining ingredients and beat with a whisk for 2 minutes.

Divide the batter among the cups and bake for 37 minutes.

Turn out of the cups and serve hot.

Tan Popovers

MAKES 6 POPOVERS

2 large eggs, at room temperature
1 cup tepid nonfat milk
2 tablespoons unsaturated oil
½ cup unbleached enriched white
   flour

½ cup whole wheat flour
¼ teaspoon salt

Proceed as for Wheat Germ Popovers, above.

Cheese Popovers

◊ *Most of the cheese flavor in these will be at the crown of the Popover.*

MAKES 6 POPOVERS

2 large eggs, at room temperature
1 cup tepid nonfat milk
2 tablespoons unsaturated oil
1 cup unbleached enriched white
flour

¼ teaspoon salt
⅜ cup grated sharp cheddar cheese

Preheat your oven to 425°F.

Grease very well six ¾-cup popover cups.

In a large bowl, beat the eggs gently with a whisk, then add the milk and oil and beat together briefly.

Add the flour and salt, and beat with a whisk for 2 minutes.

Spoon 2 tablespoons of batter into each cup, then spoon 2 rounded teaspoons of grated cheese on top of the batter in each cup. Divide the remaining batter equally among the cups. Don't worry if the cheese is not all covered.

Bake for 37 minutes.

Turn out carefully and serve hot.

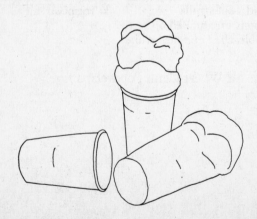

Chocolate Popovers

Who says you can't have popovers for dessert!

◊ *Most of the chocolate flavor will be near the crown of these Popovers.*

MAKES 6 POPOVERS

2 large eggs, at room temperature
1 cup tepid nonfat milk
2 tablespoons unsaturated oil
1 cup unbleached enriched white
   flour

¼ teaspoon salt
⅛ cup grated bittersweet chocolate

Preheat your oven to 425°F.

Grease very well six ¾-cup popover cups.

In a large bowl, beat the eggs briefly, then beat in the milk and oil for a moment.

Add the flour and salt and beat with a whisk for 2 minutes.

Spoon about 1 tablespoon of batter into each cup, then add 1 rounded teaspoon of grated chocolate. Divide the remaining batter equally among the cups, dripping it in to cover as much of the chocolate as possible.

Bake for only 36 minutes.

Turn out carefully and serve hot.

CROISSANTS

When we bicycled through southern France, we ate croissants from every bakery we found. Some were excellent, some stuck to the roofs of our mouths. These are great! They are not fast to make, but they are great. They are also not for anyone concerned with the amount of fat he or she eats: Each croissant contains a tablespoon of butter.

◊ *Croissants require time (about 5 hours, including chilling and rising).*

◊ *Croissants also require an efficient refrigerator. If your refrigerator runs a bit less than really cold, increase your cooling times by half.*

◊ *A marble slab works best for kneading and rolling croissants; it helps to keep the dough light and moist.*

◊ *The finished dough should be just the workable side of a batter. That is, it should spring back when you poke it, but it should be quite soft—and really too sticky to handle without a dusting of flour on your fingers.*

◊ *In this recipe, the butter starts out refrigerator-cold, and is hand-worked on baker's parchment until it is the consistency of cream cheese.* You cannot get this consistency by heating the butter: *Heating separates the butter and gives you oiliness.*

MAKES 16 CROISSANTS

1⅛ cups warm nonfat milk (about 110°F.), see page 9)
1 tablespoon honey
1 package active dry yeast
1 teaspoon salt

1 tablespoon unsaturated oil
3 cups unbleached enriched white flour
1 cup (½ pound) sweet butter

Measure the milk into a large bowl, and mix in the honey.

Add the yeast and stir. Allow to stand for a few minutes, until some yeast action begins.

Beat in the salt and oil.

Beat in 2½ cups of the flour with a wooden spoon, ½ cup at a time. Beat each ½ cup for at least 30 seconds.

Spread about ¼ cup of flour on your kneading marble, and scrape the batter out onto it.

Using floured fingers or two dough scrapers, turn dough over and over and press lightly, until you have gently worked in the flour.

When kneaded, put the dough into a clean, dry bowl—no oil—and set in a warmish place, covered, to rise until at least doubled—about 1 hour.

Meanwhile, make room in your refrigerator for the bowl of dough, and then for two trays of croissants.

When risen, flour your fingers lightly and punch down the dough. Sprinkle with a little of the remaining flour and knead in the bowl for less than a minute.

Cover with a sheet of plastic wrap, and put to cool in your refrigerator for 45 minutes to an hour until dough is cooled through.

Preparing the Butter

During the last 10 minutes of cooling, prepare the butter.

Take a sheet of baker's parchment (waxed paper will also do, but it is more fragile and might tear), and place the unwrapped cold butter on it. Break up the butter with a rolling pin, or cut it into chunks. Fold the parchment over and press the butter with the heel of your hand, to flatten it. If your hand can't do it, use the rolling pin.

Unfold the parchment, scrape the flattened butter into a pile with a dough scraper, fold over the parchment again, and press again. Keep repeating this folding, pressing, and scraping together until the butter is the texture of a thick buttercream icing. You want no oil, no wateriness, and no separation. Place the butter aside.

Rolling Out—Folding In

When the dough has chilled, sprinkle a little flour on your slab, turn the dough out onto it, flour your rolling pin, and roll the dough into a long rectangle, about ¼ inch thick.

With your fingers or a scraper, spread the butter over two thirds of the rectangle, being careful to leave an unbuttered margin of about ½ inch (see drawing A on following page).

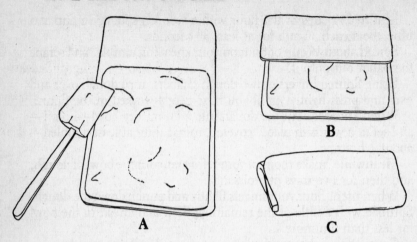

A

B

C

Fold the rectangle of buttered dough into thirds from the short side, beginning with the unbuttered section (B and C). Pinch the open edges closed (you left those unbuttered, remember). Turn the dough 90°, flour your rolling pin lightly, and roll out to a long rectangle (D), then fold into thirds again (E).

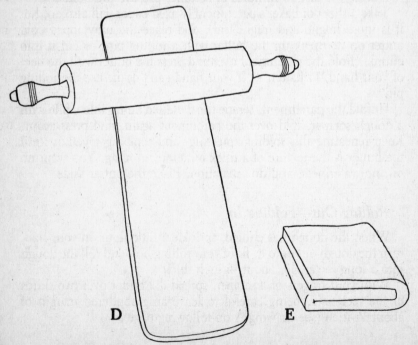

D

E

Dust the dough with a little flour, roll it in a towel, and return it to the refrigerator to chill for 1 hour.

When the dough has chilled, dust the marble with a little flour, unwrap the dough, and place it on the marble, long dimension facing away from you.

Again roll out, and fold. Turn 90 degrees, roll out, and fold again. Once more, turn and fold.

Dust the dough with a little flour, wrap again, and return to the refrigerator for another hour.

When the dough has chilled, dust the marble lightly, uncover the dough, and roll it out to a long rectangle, less than ¼ inch thick and about 9 inches wide. Cut the dough in half lengthwise, cut each half into four squares, and then cut the squares on the bias to form triangles. You should have sixteen triangles.

Dust an open space on your marble lightly for rolling.

Roll up the triangles from the wide end toward the point, pulling out and widening the croissant as you roll, as shown in Quick-Rising Crescent Rolls (page 72).

Place on two ungreased baking sheets with the point underneath to keep it from unwinding in the baking. Curve the croissant after it is placed. Leave room for plenty of rise and spread.

As you fill each sheet, place it in the refrigerator for ½ hour of final cooling.

Preheat your oven to 400°F.

Take the sheets from the refrigerator, put them directly into the oven, and bake for 10 minutes. Reduce the heat to 350°F., and bake for another 13 minutes—until the tops are golden. The bottoms will be brown and crisp and the croissants will be unbelievably flaky.

Serve directly from the oven.

BAGELS

This Jewish delicacy has become a national institution. Bagels are not haute cuisine, but they are fun. By definition, a bagel is a ring of dough, boiled in water (yes, boiled) and then baked. It must be chewy and crusty. Beyond that, the sky's the limit.

◊ *You will need a clean dish towel and a space on which to drain the bagels as they come out of the boiling water. A slotted spoon comes in handy for removing the bagels from the water.*

◊ *If you knead with a dough hook or food processor, remove the dough from the machine when the dough begins to pull away from the sides of the bowl, then finish kneading by hand.*

Sesame Basic Bagels

◊ *Unhulled sesame seeds have more flavor than hulled. If you want less seeds over all, do not turn the bagels over in the seeds.*

◊ *Of course, you can substitute poppy seeds.*

MAKES 12 BAGELS

1¼ cups hot water (about 125°F., see page 9)
2 tablespoons honey
1 package active dry yeast
2 teaspoons salt
1 large egg, at room temperature
¼ cup wheat germ
3 cups unbleached enriched white flour
4 quarts boiling water
½ cup unhulled sesame seeds

Measure the water into a large bowl. Add the honey and yeast and stir until dissolved. Allow to stand for a few minutes, until the yeast begins to foam.

Beat in the salt, egg, and wheat germ.

Beat in 2½ cups of the flour, ¼ cup at a time. Start with a whisk, but switch to a wooden spoon as the batter thickens.

Sprinkle ¼ cup of flour over the board, scrape the batter onto it, turn the batter over, and begin to work in this flour.

Knead vigorously for about 3 minutes, adding as much of the remaining ¼ cup of flour as required to get a dough that is springy and cohesive but not dry.

Pour a teaspoon of oil into the scraped-out bowl, put in the dough, and turn it a few times to oil all sides.

Put to rise, covered with a dry towel, in a very warm, draft-free place for about 30 minutes—or until the dough has risen about 50 percent.

When risen, punch down in the bowl, and knead gently for a moment to get rid of the larger bubbles. Sprinkle with a tablespoon of flour if it sticks.

Sprinkle 2 tablespoons of flour over your kneading board. Have a small amount of water handy.

Cut the dough into twelve roughly equal pieces.

Roll a piece between your palms until it is a rod about ½ inch thick and 8 to 9 inches long.

Dip one end of this rod in the water and join the ends together, with a little overlap. Make a firm join, *but do not squeeze*. You now have a ring of dough.

Put the ring on the floured board and repeat until all twelve rings are joined and on the board.

Cover the rings with a dry towel and allow to rise at room temperature (75°F. minimum) for about 15 minutes. Meanwhile, bring the 4 quarts of water to boil over a high flame, and preheat your oven to 375°F.

When they have risen, transfer four dough rings to the vigorously boiling water with a pancake turner or broad spatula.

Allow each ring to boil for 1 minute, then turn it over to boil for another minute.

Remove these four from the water gently, and put them on a towel to drain while you boil the next set. Repeat until all are boiled and draining. Handle carefully—they are hot!

Lightly grease a large cookie sheet.

Sprinkle some of the sesame seeds over a large dish, place a bagel on the seeds, then turn it over in the seeds, then place it on the greased sheet. Repeat until all are seeded and on the sheet.

Bake for about 35 minutes, or until the bottoms are brown.

Cool on a wire rack. You can eat them hot, but they are chewier cool.

Pumpernickel Bagels

MAKES 12 BAGELS

1¼ cups hot water (125°F., see page 9)
¼ cup dark molasses
1 package active dry yeast
2 teaspoons salt
1 tablespoon caraway seeds

1½ cups whole rye flour
1 cup whole wheat flour
1 to 1¼ cups unbleached enriched white flour
4 quarts boiling water

In a large bowl, combine the water, molasses, and yeast, and stir; then wait for a few minutes until the yeast action begins.

Stir in the salt and caraway seeds.

Beat in the rye and whole wheat flours, ¼ cup at a time.

Stir in ½ cup of the white flour. Sprinkle ¼ cup of white flour on the board, and scrape the batter onto the flour.

When this is worked in, knead vigorously for 5 to 6 minutes, using as much of the last ½ cup of flour as required to make a springy dough.

Proceed as for Sesame Basic Bagels, above—but omit the sesame seeds.

Onion Bagel Sticks

This is a contradiction in terms—bagels are rings, not sticks! But these zesty sticks are easier to make—and delicious.

◊ *For a little less snap, use only ½ teaspoon pepper, and 2 tablespoons of dried minced onion.*

MAKES 27 STICKS

1 cup hot water (about 125°F., see page 9)
1 package active dry yeast
2 teaspoons salt
3 tablespoons dried minced onion
1 teaspoon fresh-ground black pepper

½ cup bran
3 cups unbleached enriched white flour
4 quarts boiling water
2 tablespoons poppy seeds

Stir together the water and yeast and allow to stand for 5 minutes.

Stir in the salt, onion, pepper, and bran.

Beat in about 2¼ cups of the flour, a bit at a time. Pour ¼ cup of flour over the kneading board, scrape the batter out over it, then work the flour in.

Knead vigorously for about 4 minutes, using as much as required of the remaining ½ cup of flour to make a springy dough, on the soft side.

Pour 1 teaspoon of oil into the scraped-out bowl. Put in the dough, and turn it to oil all sides.

Rise the dough, covered with a dry towel, for about 40 minutes, in a very warm, draft-free place. When risen about 50 percent, punch the dough down, flour it lightly, and knead briefly.

Flour the kneading board and roll the dough out to a rectangle 6 by 12 inches and about ⅜ inch thick, turning and dusting with flour a few times.

Bring the 4 quarts of water to a boil, and preheat the oven to 375°F.

With a sharp knife, cut the dough into nine strips, about ¾ inch across. Cut each strip into three pieces. Separate slightly on the floured board, and allow to rise for about 15 minutes.

With a spatula, put six sticks at a time into the boiling water. Boil about 1 minute per side, and drain on a dish towel. Handle them gently, going in and coming out.

Grease a large cookie sheet, and transfer all the sticks to the one sheet.

Sprinkle with poppy seeds, then bake for about 35 minutes.

Cool on a wire rack.

Tan Raisin Bagels

The raisins and honey give these bagels a delightfully sweet taste.

◊ *Chop the raisins in a blender or food processor with a few tablespoons of flour, so they don't stick to the blades or the container.*

MAKES 12 BAGELS

1 cup hot water (about 125°F., see page 9)
¼ cup honey
1 package active dry yeast
1 large egg, at room temperature
1½ teaspoons salt

½ cup chopped unsulfured raisins
1 cup whole wheat flour
3 cups unbleached enriched white flour
4 quarts boiling water

Combine the water, honey, and yeast in a large bowl. Stir well, then wait a few minutes until yeast action begins.

Stir in the egg, salt, and raisins.

Beat in the whole wheat flour, ½ cup at a time.

Beat in 2½ cups of the white flour, ¼ cup at a time.

Sprinkle ¼ cup of white flour onto the board, gently work in this flour, and then knead vigorously for about 5 minutes, using as much of the remaining ¼ cup as required to make a springy dough.

Then proceed as for Sesame Basic Bagels (page 202), omitting the sesame seeds.

～⌒⌒ 13 ⌒～

Quick Breads

THESE are mix-and-bake breads—that's what makes them "quick." They take just as long in the oven as kneaded breads, but eliminating kneading and rising saves a lot of time.

Quick breads are risen by chemical action, with baking soda and/or baking powder (see page 6). They are generally started in a cold oven, and then baked at temperatures a little cooler than those used for most kneaded breads to give the chemical reactions time to work to their fullest.

Most quick breads are dessert breads. But you could make any of these recipes less sweet, to your own taste, or remove the fruits or nuts and make a Quick Sandwich Bread.

Irish Soda Bread is a soda-risen bread, but it is kneaded, so we have included it in Chapter 7, Ethnic and Holiday Fancy Breads. Muffins and biscuits, which are also quick breads, have their own chapters.

◊ *If, in your experimentation with various ingredients, you wind up with a bread that is too low and too wet, increase the amount of flour dramatically—by as much as a third.*

◊ *If you want to save even more time, you can premeasure a recipe's dry ingredients and store in the refrigerator, then add the wet ones when baking time comes.*

◊ *Non-sodium baking powder can be found in health food stores. It contains no salt and no aluminum, but you have to use about 50 percent more to get the same rise.*

Apple-Walnut Loaf

This is a true dessert bread: sweet and satisfying. We give it here in two versions. Version I is our original calories-be-damned recipe, the one created for our bread-baking classes. Version II is a lower-calorie-but-still-delicious recipe. Aside from the calories, the versions are equally nutritious.

◊ *Make certain your vanilla is fresh and strong—and real vanilla extract, not vanillin. It makes a difference in the final flavor, especially in Version II.*
◊ *Wash but do not peel the apple—the skin adds to the character of the bread.*

MAKES 2 LOAVES IN 7½-INCH PANS

Version I

½ cup unsaturated oil
1 cup honey
1 teaspoon vanilla
4 rounded tablespoons yogurt
2 large eggs, at room temperature
1 teaspoon baking soda
½ teaspoon salt
2 cups whole wheat flour
1 cup walnuts, coarsely chopped
1 medium apple, cored, chunked small

Version II

¼ cup unsaturated oil
¾ cup honey
½ cup minus 2 tablespoons water
2 teaspoons vanilla
4 rounded tablespoons yogurt
2 large eggs, at room temperature
1 teaspoon baking soda
½ teaspoon salt
2 cups whole wheat flour
1 cup walnuts, coarsely chopped
1 medium apple, cored, chunked small

Combine all the liquid ingredients in a large bowl and mix well.
Stir in the soda and salt.
Mix the flour in well, then the walnuts and apple chunks.
Grease two 7½-inch loaf pans well and divide the batter between them. You *must* grease the pans well or the bread may stick.

Starting in a cold oven set for 350°F., bake for about 50 to 60 minutes, or until the bread knife-tests done (page 7). Because of the water, Version II will take a few minutes longer to bake than Version I.

Since the apple stays moist, it will leave streaks on your knife when you test. Don't mistake apple for batter. Apple wipes off easily.

Allow to cool for a few minutes before you remove the loaves from the pans, and then finish the cooling on a wire rack—but serve hot, when the flavor is best.

Date-Nut Bread

This bread has a full, sweet flavor: It is the sweetest bread we bake. If you want to quiet it down a bit, cut back to 1 cup of dates. But we prefer to use the 2 cups, and serve it sliced thin.

◊ *To grind the dates, put into the blender or food processor with some flour (we divide the dates into three batches and use 3 tablespoons of the flour from the recipe with each batch) and process briefly. The flour keeps the dates from sticking to the blades or container.*

MAKES 2 LOAVES IN 7½-INCH PANS

2 cups (1 pound) moist pitted dates
2 cups whole wheat flour
1 cup coarsely chopped walnuts
1½ cups yogurt
2 large eggs, at room temperature

2 tablespoons unsaturated oil
¼ cup honey
2 teaspoons baking soda
¼ cup warm water

Grind the dates with some of the flour.

Scrape into a large bowl, and add the rest of the flour and the walnuts.

In a separate bowl, mix together the yogurt, eggs, oil, and honey until smooth. Pour over the date mixture and stir until evenly mixed.

Grease two 7½-inch loaf pans.

Dissolve the baking soda in the water, add to the batter, and stir in well.

Immediately, spoon into the baking pans, put into a cold oven set at 350°F., and bake for about 1 hour—or until the loaves test done (see page 7).

Cool briefly in the pans, then turn out. Serve hot.

Banana Bread

Our Banana Bread is a delicious variation on the traditional favorite—it contains fresh mint! If you don't like (or don't have) fresh mint, then just drop it from the recipe. Even without the mint, the bread is great.

◇ *To keep the bread moist, do not overbake.*
◇ *We mix all the liquid ingredients together in our blender. If you don't have a blender (or food processor) make certain you mash the banana quite well and mix all the liquids (and the mint) thoroughly.*

MAKES 2 LOAVES IN 7½-INCH PANS

2 cups unbleached enriched white flour
2 cups whole wheat flour
2 teaspoons baking soda
2 large eggs, at room temperature

¼ cup chopped fresh mint
¾ cup yogurt
2 teaspoons vanilla extract
1½ cups ripe mashed bananas (about 2 large bananas)

Preheat your oven to 375°F.

Measure the flours and baking soda into a large bowl, and mix well.

In a separate bowl, combine the rest of the ingredients and mix until fairly uniform.

Grease well two 7½-inch loaf pans.

Pour the liquid ingredients into the dry, and stir until well mixed—but as briefly as you can.

Divide the batter into the 2 pans and bake for 50 to 55 minutes, or until the loaves knife-test done (see page 7). When you test, remember that the banana stays moist and will stain the testing knife.

Expect the loaves to make lots of rise.

Turn out and cool on a wire rack. Serve warm.

Time 1 - added sugar too dry used 2½ bananas need more 3-4

212 □ BAKE YOUR OWN BREAD

Boston Brown Bread

Boston Brown Bread is a *steamed* bread. It is put into closed containers (molds or cans), the containers are half-immersed in water, and the water is then brought to a boil and kept at a boil for from 1 hour to 3 hours—depending on the size of the containers.

This is a strong-flavored bread—the molasses makes it so. But it is grand when spread with a bit of cream cheese or cottage cheese. We have even used it as a breakfast "cereal," broken up in some yogurt. Delicious!

◇ *This bread slices poorly when hot—but it tastes best when hot. For hot slices, cut with a piece of strong thread or unwaxed dental floss. Loop the thread levelly around the loaf, cross the ends, and slowly and gently pull the ends apart. Very neat.*

MAKES 3 LOAVES IN 1-POUND COFFEE CANS,
OR 1 LARGE LOAF IN A 3-QUART MOLD

1 cup whole wheat flour	2 teasoons baking soda
1 cup cornmeal	1 cup seedless unsulfured raisins
1 cup rye flour	1½ cups yogurt
1 teaspoon salt	1 cup dark molasses

stone ground

Into a large bowl, measure the whole wheat flour, cornmeal, rye flour, salt, baking soda, and raisins, and mix well.

In a separate bowl, mix together the yogurt and molasses, then add them to the dry ingredients and mix until uniform.

Grease the desired molds very well: three 1-pound coffee cans, or one 3-quart mold, or one 2-quart mold plus one smaller (soup-can size) can, or whatever combination you choose.

Spoon the batter in, filling no more than two thirds of the way. Cover with aluminum foil.

Put a rack into the bottom of a large pot to just hold the molds above the pot bottom. Set the molds on the rack and pour in hot water until it comes halfway up the molds. Cover the pot.

Bring to a boil and continue boiling for the time indicated, adding hot water as needed. A 1-pound coffee can will take about 1½ hours, a smaller can (soup-can size) about 1 hour; a large mold without a center post about 3 hours, a mold with a center post about 1½ hours.

When the loaves test done with a toothpick (see page 7), tap out of the molds, allow to cool on a wire rack, and serve warm.

Maple-Pecan Bread

This tan bread is moist and delicious. To keep it that way, be careful not to overcook it.

◊ *The pecans should be very coarse—halves broken into four parts. And the maple syrup must be real maple, not maple-flavored syrup.*

MAKES 2 LOAVES IN 7-INCH PANS

2 large eggs, at room temperature
1 cup maple syrup
¼ cup unsaturated oil
½ cup yogurt
grated zest of 1 lemon
juice of 1 lemon
1 cup coarsely chopped pecans

2 cups whole wheat flour
1 cup unbleached enriched white flour
2 teaspoons baking soda
¼ cup warm water
8 extra pecan halves (for garnish)

In a large mixing bowl, combine the eggs, syrup, oil, yogurt, zest, and lemon juice, and beat until smooth.

Stir in the chopped pecans.

Measure in the flours and stir until all moist.

Grease two 7-inch loaf pans.

Dissolve the soda in the water, then pour it over the batter and stir in well.

Divide the batter between the two pans, then space out 4 pecan halves over each top.

Starting in a cold oven set at 375°F., bake for 40 minutes, or until the loaves knife-test done (see page 7).

Allow to cool briefly in the pans, then turn out and cool on a wire rack. Serve warm.

Carrot Bread

Vegetable breads are made for their special moisture and texture.

◊ *We use only fresh-ground nutmeg. The whole nutmegs keep virtually forever and grate up very easily on a small grater. There is no comparison between fresh-ground and packaged-ground nutmeg. Just watch out for your knuckles.*

◊ *The carrots and yogurt can be grated together in the blender or processor.*

MAKES 2 LOAVES IN 7-INCH PANS

2½ cups whole wheat flour
½ cup brown sugar
½ teaspoon salt
½ teaspoon powdered ginger
1 teaspoon fresh-ground nutmeg
½ cup chopped pecans
½ cup unsulfured raisins

zest of 1 lemon
1 cup yogurt
2 medium carrots, washed, trimmed, and grated
2 teaspoons baking soda
½ cup warm water

Into a large bowl, measure the flour, sugar, salt, ginger, nutmeg, pecans, and raisins. Grate in the zest. Mix well.

Stir in the yogurt and carrots until everything is wet.

Grease well two 7-inch loaf pans.

Dissolve the soda in the water, then mix it well into the rest of the batter. Do not beat.

Divide the batter between the two pans and, starting in a cold oven set at 375°F., bake for about 35 minutes, or until the loaves test done (see page 7).

Turn out, cool briefly on a wire rack, and serve hot.

Cranberry-Orange Bread

We do most of the work for this bread in the blender (a food processor works just as well), and the sequence of ingredients assumes that you will, too.

◊ *Use only fresh (or fresh-frozen) cranberries. We usually freeze a few pounds at Thanksgiving time for summer baking.*

MAKES 3 LOW LOAVES IN 7-INCH PANS

zest of 1 orange
1 cup yogurt
½ cup honey
1 large egg, at room temperature
1 cup raw cranberries
½ cup dried shredded coconut

2½ cups whole wheat flour
¼ cup wheat germ
¼ cup bran
2 teaspoons baking soda
¼ cup warm water

Cut the zest into pieces and grind it in the blender.

Add the yogurt, honey, and egg, and blend until smooth.

Add the cranberries, and blend until well chopped.

Add the coconut and blend in briefly.

Measure the flour, wheat germ, and bran into a bowl, add the contents of the blender, and mix gently until all wet. At this stage the batter has an awful purple color.

Allow to stand while you grease three 7-inch loaf pans well.

Dissolve the soda in the warm water, then stir into the batter, mixing well, but gently.

Divide the batter among the pans and, starting in a cold oven set for 375°F., bake for 35 to 40 minutes, or until the loaves test done (see page 7).

Turn out and cool on a wire rack. Serve warm.

Blueberry Rice Bread

Rice flour has an unusually smooth texture, especially when used, as it is here, without any wheat flour at all. If you have, or a member of your family has, an allergy to wheat, this delicious loaf can be a great help.

◊ *Either fresh or thawed frozen berries can be used—and don't hesitate to substitute raspberries or cut-up strawberries.*

MAKES 2 LOAVES IN 7½-INCH PANS

2½ cups brown rice flour
2 teaspoons baking soda
2 large eggs, at room temperature
¾ cup yogurt
½ cup honey
1 cup blueberries

Grease well two 7½-inch loaf pans.

Measure the flour and soda into a large bowl and mix well.

In a separate bowl, combine the eggs well, add the yogurt and honey, and stir until smooth. Stir in the blueberries.

Combine the two mixtures, mixing well, then divide between the two pans.

Starting in a cold oven set for 350°F., bake, for 40 to 45 minutes, or until the loaf knife-tests done (see page 7). When testing, remember that the berries will always be moist and leave moisture (which wipes off readily) on your testing knife.

Cool briefly in the pans, then turn out and cool on a wire rack.

～◎14◎～

Biscuits

BISCUITS are easy. Not as easy as muffins and quick breads, but they usually elicit more compliments than a loaf of kneaded bread with a tiny fraction of the trouble and work. And they can be ready in half an hour, or less, from the urge. (In fact, it usually takes 15 minutes for our oven to preheat to the required 400°F. and only 12 minutes for us to prepare the biscuit dough.)

Biscuits are American. Wherever you go in this country, you meet regional varieties: We found the Sour Cream Biscuit in Pennsylvania-Dutch country; Southerners consider Buttermilk Biscuits as their own special property.

Biscuits are marvelous for experimentation. Once you have the basic ideas, it is hard to fail with them. The worst that can happen is that you won't get as much rise as you would like. They'll still taste great.

◇ *Each biscuit recipe calls for a specific amount of flour. You will also need a few extra tablespoons of flour for the board in order to roll out the dough.*

◇ *If you wish to substitute nonsodium, nonaluminum baking powder, increase the amount called for by 50 percent.*

◇ *You will need a biscuit cutter between 2½ and 3 inches in diameter. It can be a small glass or it can be an antique. The biscuits won't care.*

◇ *You can use a rolling pin to roll out the dough, or you can press it into a flattened shape with the palms of your hands.*

217

◊ *You can make your biscuits more nutritious by the substitution of bran, wheat germ, or whole wheat flour. Or make them more attractive (and tasty) by the addition of chopped nuts or seeds, or dried fruit—such as raisins, dates, cherries, apples, even chopped papaya.*

Sour Cream Biscuits

Sour cream has changed a lot since we were kids. For one thing, it is considerably lower in butterfat than it used to be. Sour cream used to be cream that was cultured and tasted sour. Some of it still is. But most of it isn't.

Most of the sour cream on the market today (and we are not talking about sour cream substitutes which must be labeled as such) is made mostly from cultured *milk*—a lot lower in butterfat. In fact, we bought a sour cream the other day that was made entirely from cultured *low-fat milk* (with rennet to thicken it). The flavor is the same, but the butterfat is way down. You can use any kind of sour cream in this recipe.

A second change in sour cream has nothing to do with the ingredients, but involves the measurements. Years ago, sour cream was sold by volume: pints, quarts, half pints. Today, it is sold by the pound. A pint (2 cups) of water is a pound, but *a pound of sour cream is less than 2 cups*. That's because sour cream is heavier than water. What difference does it make? The recipe below calls for 1 cup of sour cream. A pound of sour cream does not give you quite enough for two batches. Sorry about that.

◊ *To make* Wheat Germ *or* Bran Sour Cream Biscuits, *substitute ¼ cup of wheat germ or bran for ¼ cup of white flour.*
◊ *To make* Tan Sour Cream Biscuits, *substitute ½ cup of whole wheat flour for ½ cup of white flour. Since whole wheat flour is more absorbent than white, you will also need to add an extra tablespoon or two of sour cream.*

MAKES 12 BISCUITS

2 cups unbleached enriched white flour	½ teaspoon baking soda
2 teaspoons baking powder	1 cup sour cream

Preheat your oven to 400°F.

Put the flour, baking powder, and baking soda into a large bowl and mix until uniform.

Spoon the sour cream over the surface in tablespoon-size globs, and stir in thoroughly. Do not knead.

Sprinkle some flour on the kneading board and scrape out the dough onto it, then flour your hands and pat the dough flat.

Turn and pat, spreading the flour on the board so the batter does not stick. Press the batter flat (or roll it out with a floured pin) until it is fairly level and about ½ inch thick.

Grease a large baking sheet.

Cut out as many biscuits as you can with a biscuit cutter. Do not place your cutter at the very edge of the dough: The edges tend to be thinner, and thinner dough makes thinner biscuits.

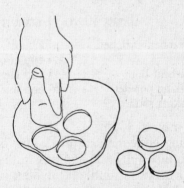

Place the cut-outs on the sheet, allowing a little space between.

When you have cut as many as you can, gather the leftover dough together, reflatten it, and cut out some more. Continue until you have only a small amount of dough left, and shape that last biscuit by hand.

Bake for about 15 minutes, or until the tops are lightly browned and the bottoms are golden.

Tan Tea Biscuits

A tea biscuit is a sweet biscuit with dried fruit and perhaps chopped nuts. This basic recipe is delightful on a number of counts. The orange juice sweetens the biscuit slightly, and gives the batter a lovely creamy color. The nuts provide a pleasant crunch, and the dates make for a sweet and unusual flavor.

◊ *For tasty variations, substitute unsulfured raisins for the dates, and/or peanuts for the walnuts. You can also substitute pineapple juice for the orange juice. If you don't want a nutty crunch, use ½ cup of fruit and no nuts.*

◊ *To substitute peanuts, simply grind ¼ cup of unsalted shelled peanuts and added to the batter. If you grind the peanuts in a blender or food processor, this creates some peanut flour, so you will need to increase the amount of fruit juice by 2 tablespoons.*

MAKES 10 TO 11 BISCUITS

1½ cups unbleached enriched
   white flour
½ cup whole wheat flour
3 teaspoons baking powder
¾ teaspoon baking soda
pinch salt
¼ cup chopped walnuts
¼ cup chopped dates
¾ cup orange juice

Preheat your oven to 400°F.

Into a mixing bowl measure the flours, baking powder, baking soda, and salt; mix well. Add and mix in the walnuts and dates.

Add the juice and stir until all the flour is wet.

Pour a few tablespoons of flour onto the kneading board, scrape the batter onto it, and flatten the batter with your floured hands, or roll out with a floured rolling pin. Turn the batter over and pat, or roll, to about ½ inch thick.

Cut out biscuits 2¼ inch across and place on a greased baking sheet. (If you would prefer a biscuit that looks more like a bun, tuck the edges of the cut-out biscuit under and reflatten somewhat between your floured hands.)

Bake for 14 to 16 minutes, until the bottoms are brown.

Wheat Germ Milk Biscuits

The nicest part of milk biscuits is that one always has milk in the house, either as whole or nonfat liquid milk, or as powdered milk to be reconstituted.

◊ *To make* Bran Milk Biscuits *or* Tan Milk Biscuits, *substitute ¼ cup of bran or ½ cup of whole wheat flour for an equal amount of white flour.*

MAKES 12 BISCUITS

1¾ cups unbleached enriched
    white flour
¼ cup wheat germ

3 teaspoons baking powder
¾ cup milk

Preheat the oven to 400°F.

Combine the ingredients in a bowl and mix until uniform, then proceed as for Sour Cream Biscuits, page 218.

Cheese Wheat Germ Biscuits

We find a sharp or extra-sharp cheddar best for this recipe. If you object to the orange spots, there are uncolored cheddars.

MAKES 12 TO 14 BISCUITS

1¾ cups unbleached enriched
    white flour
¼ cup wheat germ

4 teaspoons baking powder
¾ cup grated cheese
1 cup milk

Preheat your oven to 400°F.

Combine the flour, wheat germ, and baking powder in a large bowl and mix until uniform.

Stir in the cheese well.

Add the milk, stir until all the dry ingredients are wet, and then proceed as for Sour Cream Biscuits, page 218.

Bran Buttermilk Biscuits

Buttermilk is supposed to give you the best biscuits. Buttermilk Biscuits certainly are delicious, and they rise high, but to us they are not as special in taste or texture as the Sour Cream Biscuits (page 218). However, they are lower in fat.

Buttermilk is the "milk" left over after the making of butter. It has as little fat as skim milk does, but a culture has been introduced into it for sour flavor.

◊ *For* Wheat Germ Buttermilk Biscuits, *substitute ¼ cup of wheat germ for ¼ cup of white flour. For* Tan Buttermilk Biscuits, *substitute ½ cup of whole wheat for ½ cup of white.*

◊ *If you want a flakier* Rich Buttermilk Biscuit, *add 2 tablespoons of sweet butter. Work the butter in with a pastry knife or by mashing it with a whisk, or by rubbing bits of it into the flour between your fingers. If you add the butter, you should reduce the amount of buttermilk by 1 tablespoon.*

◊ *Do not substitute yogurt for the buttermilk—yogurt does not make a flaky biscuit.*

MAKES 12 BISCUITS

1¾ cups unbleached enriched
white flour
¼ cup fresh bran
2 teaspoons baking powder

½ teaspoon baking soda
¾ cup plus 2 tablespoons buttermilk

Preheat the oven to 400°F.

Measure the dry ingredients into a bowl and stir them until uniform.

Pour in the buttermilk, mix until all the flour is wet, then continue as for Sour Cream Biscuits, page 218.

∽❤15❤∽

Muffins

MUFFINS are the quickest of the quick breads. They are simple to mix up, and soon out of the oven.

We have given only a few interesting recipes here, but don't be limited by them. Use them as a springboard to create your own. Let us know if you come up with something great.

All of these recipes are baked in foil muffin liners. However, if you are going to experiment with various ingredients for muffins, you may want to use a nonstick pan*—sometimes muffins with exotic ingredients or whole-grain flours will stick to even foil papers.

◇ *To save even more time, mix up the dry ingredients beforehand and store in the refrigerator, then add the wet ingredients when it is time to bake.*

◇ *Muffins are raised by baking powder. If you wish to substitute a nonsodium, nonaluminum baking powder, increase the amount by 50 percent.*

◇ *When you combine the dry and wet ingredients, mix no more than necessary to wet everything thoroughly. Extra beating can develop gluten—and we wish to avoid that.*

---

* Muffins (and sometimes drop rolls) are the only cooking that we do in nonstick pans, and then we use a 12-muffin "Baker's Secret" pan from EKCO. We have used it and washed it scores of times with no visible degrading of the nonstick surface—which makes us believe that we ingest very little of it with our muffins.

Banana-Bran-Nut Muffins

◇ *We use the blender to mash the banana to get it into smaller bits than casual mashing with a fork will do. (A food processor does the same job.) If you use a fork, mash and mix a lot.*

◇ *If you prefer honey to brown sugar, make a straight substitution. No other adjustment is necessary.*

MAKES 12 MUFFINS

1¼ cups bran	3 tablespoons brown sugar
1¼ cups whole wheat flour	¾ cup chopped walnuts
1½ teaspoons baking soda	2 tablespoons unsaturated oil
1 teaspoon baking powder	1¼ cups yogurt
¼ teaspoon salt	1 overripe banana

Preheat your oven to 400°F.

Put a dozen foil muffin liners into a muffin pan.

In a large bowl combine the bran, whole wheat flour, baking soda, baking powder, salt, sugar, and walnuts, and stir until well mixed.

Measure the oil and yogurt into the blender (or processor), and add the banana, broken up. Blend at medium speed until uniform, then pour over the dry ingredients.

Stir gently until all is wet.

Spoon the batter into the foil papers and bake for about 20 minutes. Test for doneness as you would test a bread (see page 7), but be aware that banana may masquerade as uncooked batter. (Banana wipes off more easily than dough.)

Carob Chip Muffins

◊ *Carob chips are found in health food stores. Chocolate chips can be substituted for the carob chips in equal measure.*

MAKES 16 MUFFINS

2 cups unbleached enriched
   white flour
¼ cup wheat germ
1 teaspoon baking powder
1 teaspoon baking soda
freshly grated zest of ½ lemon

1 cup carob chips
¼ cup unsaturated oil
¼ cup honey
1 cup yogurt
2 large eggs, at room temperature

Preheat your oven to 400°F.

Put sixteen foil muffin liners into muffin pans.

Mix the dry ingredients and the zest in a large bowl until fairly uniform.

In another bowl, combine the remaining ingredients and beat until smooth.

Pour the wet ingredients over the dry and stir gently until just damp.

Divide the batter among the foil liners and bake for about 15 minutes, or until they test done with a toothpick (see page 7).

Cornmeal-Date Muffins

These delicious muffins take their place at the head of the taste parade.

◊ *To chop dates in a blender or food processor, measure in a few tablespoons of the flour, then add the pitted dates, and process until chopped. To chop the dates by hand, pour those few tablespoons of flour onto a cutting board, roll the dates in the flour, and chop. Be sure, in both cases, all the flour goes into the recipe.*

MAKES 12 MUFFINS

½ cup pitted dates, packed
½ cup whole wheat flour
1½ cups yellow cornmeal
½ teaspoon salt
1 tablespoon baking powder

¼ cup unsaturated vegetable oil
½ cup nonfat milk
3 tablespoons honey
2 large eggs, at room temperature

Preheat your oven to 400°F.

Put twelve foil muffin liners into a muffin pan.

Chop the dates with the whole wheat flour and put into a large mixing bowl.

Add the cornmeal, salt, and baking powder, and stir until fairly uniform.

Into another bowl, measure the oil, milk, and honey, and break in the eggs. Stir with a fork until smooth.

Pour the wet ingredients over the dry, and stir gently until all is wet.

Divide the batter among the foil liners, and bake for about 15 minutes, or until one tests done with a toothpick (see page 7).

Corn-Bran-Raisin Muffins

◊ *If your raisins are small, use them whole; if they are large, chop with the whole wheat flour as described in Cornmeal-Date Muffins (page 226).*

MAKES 12 MUFFINS

1½ cups yellow cornmeal
½ cup bran
½ cup whole wheat flour
½ teaspoon salt
1 teaspoon baking powder
1 teaspoon baking soda

½ cup unsulfured raisins
¼ cup unsaturated oil
¾ cup yogurt
¼ cup honey
2 large eggs, at room temperature

Preheat your oven to 400°F.

Put twelve foil muffin liners into a muffin pan.

In a large mixing bowl, combine the cornmeal, bran, flour, salt, baking powder, baking soda, and raisins, and stir until well mixed.

Combine the remaining ingredients in a separate bowl, and stir gently with a fork until uniform.

Divide the batter among the foil liners, and bake for about 15 minutes, or until a muffin tests done with a toothpick (see page 7).

Bran Drops

These small muffins are quick to make—and quick to disappear at the table.

◊ *The flavor of the molasses comes through here (aided by the bran), so if you don't like molasses, switch to honey.*

◊ *These "drops" are so small that they do not require the support of a muffin pan. If you want, you can just put the foil muffin liners in cake pans.*

MAKES 18 DROPS

1 cup bran
1 cup whole wheat flour
½ teaspoon salt
4 teaspoons baking powder

¾ cup nonfat milk
2 tablespoons unsaturated oil
2 tablespoons molasses

Preheat your oven to 400°F.

Measure the dry ingredients into a large bowl and stir until well mixed.

Add the wet ingredients and stir until fairly uniform.

Spoon a rounded tablespoon of batter into each of eighteen foil muffin liners and bake for 14 minutes, or until the tops are crisp and the bottoms are somewhat browned. Don't test—taste. And don't overbake.

~✺16✺~

Keeping Bread and Dough

BREAD

People are not surprised that a home-baked bread tastes better than store-bought: They expect that. What surprises them is how well these breads *keep*.

Actually, it should not be so surprising. For one thing, home-baked bread is eaten much sooner than a commercial bread would be. More important, commercial breads are kneaded in machines which force air into them—which is why so many of them seem to have no substance and dry out so quickly.

Also, if commercial bakers used honey (which is a natural preservative) and the fresher, more wholesome ingredients you can use at home, they would have no need for chemical preservatives.

Freezing

The best way to keep bread for more than a day is to freeze it.

Bread is among the easiest and safest of foods to freeze, even for extended periods of time—up to a year, according to the U.S. Department of Agriculture (USDA).

Stored wrapped tightly in aluminum foil, there is virtually no loss of taste, texture, or wholesomeness in the frozen loaf. And, if you put it in the oven to reheat, it will come out tasting like the next best thing to fresh-baked.

To prepare bread for freezing, first, let it cool to room temperature on a wire rack. During this cooling, whatever water vapor is being evaporated from the hot loaf dissipates into the air before you wrap it. This minimizes water touching (and wetting) the crust.

Next, wrap the bread tightly in aluminum foil and put it in the freezer. Then, on the happy day when you decide to eat it, just put the loaf, foil and all, into the oven, and bake at about 400°F. for 10 minutes (or until the center is warm). It's amazing how good a loaf can be, even if it has been in your freezer for months.

Or, when the fresh-baked loaf is cool, slice as thin as pleases you, gather the slices together into the loaf shape, and then wrap. When you wish to, remove as many slices as you want, and toast them. The loaf gets rewrapped and returned to the freezer.

If toast is what you like, frozen is indistinguishable from fresh.

One thing about frozen bread: once thawed, it tends to dry out faster than fresh bread.

The Refrigerator Versus the Bread Box

A bread gets "stale" (hard), as it loses its moisture. The moisture evaporates into the air while the solid ingredients stay where they are, getting drier and drier, and harder and harder.

A bread gets "moldy" because the microorganisms of this world find moist places (like bread) a good home.

These two problems, staleness and mold, are the two big difficulties in keeping bread fresh outside of the freezer.

Believe it or not, bread retains its moisture best if it is kept quite warm. According to the USDA, bread will keep soft "indefinitely" at 140°F. Now that is warm. Just how would you do it? And if you could do it, how would you keep the mold away? Mold absolutely loves temperatures like that.

The USDA also says that bread will keep soft for 100 hours (about four days) at 110°F. Also a nice breeding temperature for mold.

At 70°F., room temperature, breads keep soft for 40 hours (less than 2 days!).

How about putting bread into the refrigerator? That's why we have refrigerators, isn't it? to inhibit the growth of microorganisms. At 32°F., you can expect your bread to stay soft (fresh) for all of 10 hours!

That last figure came as a shock to us. We had been taught at our mothers' knees to put unused bread in the refrigerator to keep it fresh. And now the federal government was telling us that our moms were misinformed and that if we put the bread in the refrigerator, we were just hurrying it to staleness.

So, any bread that is not being frozen is best kept in a bread box. This will keep your breads at room temperature or slightly higher, and free from dust and creatures, and soft for a couple of days—though it does nothing for the problem of mold.

Keeping Power

Breads vary greatly in keeping power. Those made with water get stale quickest. Honey will help a water bread keep its moisture (honey absorbs moisture from the air—your jar of honey will absorb moisture and thin out if you don't keep the jar tightly closed, especially in humid weather), and if you use enough honey you can keep a bread for weeks.

Shortening (oils) of any kind will help a bread stay moist (you know the way a drop of oil just won't dry out). The more shortening in a bread, the longer it will stay moist.

Of the breads in this book, brioches are the richest in oil; so oily that we can keep our treasure trove of *Petites Brioches* in a plastic bag in the refrigerator for as long as 2 or 3 weeks without their going dry. At any weak moment, we just pop one or two into our ancient top-of-the-stove potato baker (for the more modern among you, a toasting oven would also do), and, *voilà*, almost like fresh baked.

But with any bread that uses shortening you run into another problem: rancidity.

Never eat anything rancid—even if only the slightest bit. Rancid oils will destroy vitamins, and they can also make you quite sick. So, if something smells off, throw it out. The money loss is not to be compared to the health loss.

Any oil-and-egg-rich breads not eaten the first day must be kept in the refrigerator, where they—unlike water breads—keep quite well without going hard.

Wrapping Still-Warm Breads

As for plastic bags, if still-warm breads are put in plastic, their crusts are softened by their own moisture. We like our crusts crusty, so if warm bread is to be kept overnight, or to be given to friends, we put it into a brown paper bag, folding the top several times to make it creature proof, and let it get one day "stale" to protect the crust. Brown paper lets all the moisture out and keeps the bread clean and dust-free.

Reviving Stale Bread

In one sense a bread begins to go stale as soon as you put it in the oven. The very process of baking involves moisture loss. (For proof, weigh your loaf before and after baking.) Your nose also confirms this. When breads get done, their odors become very strong—that's one of the indicators that a bread may be ready to come out of the oven. That odor is the result of evaporation—you smell the bread because of the moisture particles in the air.

Reviving stale bread involves trying to retrieve some of the lost moisture. Sprinkle a little water over the dry bread and then place it in the oven (or toaster oven), just until the moisture approaches its original level.

DOUGH

Unbaked dough is more perishable than bread. Its life in the refrigerator is about 2 to 3 weeks and its life in the freezer is about 2 to 3 months. But if your freezer will not keep ice cream quite hard, don't plan to keep your dough in it for more than a month.

We have kept dough in the refrigerator for over a month, then baked it, to find ourselves with a good texture but an unpleasantly "winey" flavor. This "wineyness" comes from the continued action of the yeast. The refrigerator slows the yeast, but doesn't stop it.

Dough stored in the refrigerator should be in a bowl covered with a piece of plastic. The dough will rise and fall in the bowl, and on the rise it may push off its plastic cover. Do check periodically, and recover it: If allowed to be uncovered it will dry out and pick up the odors of the refrigerator.

Dough stored in the freezer should be put into a plastic bag, loosely closed but not sealed. The dough will swell until it has frozen solid; if the bag is airtight, it might burst. After the dough freezes, squeeze the air out of the bag and seal it well with a twist-tie.

Bring the ball of dough out of the freezer about 2 hours before you want to work it.

If you want to freeze shaped unrisen loaves or rolls, just wrap them in greased plastic wrap and put them in. Doughs with seeds actually improve in flavor with a freezing.

On baking day, a full-sized loaf will take 5 to 6 hours to thaw and rise; you can save time by moving the frozen loaf to the refrigerator the night before.

Rolls take only 2 hours to thaw and rise.

Glossary

This is a collection of definitions, descriptions, and explanations of the terms, techniques, and ingredients we use in this book, as we use them. It is intended as a supplement to Chapter 1—Techniques and Ingredients.

ALMOND PASTE   A combination of finely ground almonds and sweeteners, it is the main ingredient in marzipan.

BAGUETTE   From the French for "rod," *baguette* has come to mean any loaf that starts its life as a rod-shaped piece of dough. This is the traditional shape of French bread.

BAKER'S PARCHMENT   Also called Kitchen Parchment. This silicone-impregnated paper is very handy stuff, serving a multitude of purposes in the kitchen. It is used as is waxed paper, but without wax melting or scraping off and getting into your food. Cookies can be baked directly on it, without greasing the cookie sheet; it can be used to line loaf pans for breads or cakes; it can be used as a work surface (one chef of our acquaintance uses it for chopping chocolate for mousse); or it can be shaped into a Cornet (see page 236) for use as a onetime pastry bag.

We have bought it in gourmet shops, but found it only once in a supermarket, and that in a small package at a relatively high price. We have been successful, however, at hustling parchment. Sometimes, if it is not to be found on the shelf, a request at the bakery of your supermarket (if your supermarket bakes its own bread) will elicit half a dozen sheets of parchment, free.

BAKER'S PEEL   If you have seen a pizza baker make pizza, you have seen a peel: it is that long-handled flat paddle that he uses to insert

234

and remove the whole pies. Baker's peels have various lengths of handle, and while they are usually made of wood, we have seen them lately of aluminum.

BAKING SHEET   A large flat metal pan with a lip all the way around.

BASE   An alkaline substance—the opposite of acid. A base (such as baking soda) is brought into contact with an acid (such as yogurt) in a batter, to create the bubbles that rise some breads.

BOWL SCRAPER   See *Dough Scraper*.

BROMINATING   The forcing of bromine gas through flour as a preservative. Many large-scale processors of whole wheat flour brominate their product to increase its shelf life. If a flour is not brominated, it must be refrigerated. However, brominating kills the wheat germ.

CANDIED FRUIT   See *Dried Fruit*.

CANDY THERMOMETER   A long glass tube designed to measure the temperature of sugar water as it heats through various stages on the way to making candy. At the lower end of its scale, it is very handy for checking out the temperature of any liquid before it is added to a yeast recipe.

CAROB   Also called St. John's bread. The large seed pods of the *Ceretonia siliqua* tree (a tender broad-leafed evergreen of the pea family that is native to the Mediterranean). These edible pods are sold whole or ground up into a flour. Carob is naturally sweet and a nutritionally acceptable substitute for chocolate. Chocolate is naturally bitter and must have sugar added to bring it to what most folks accept as the real taste of chocolate. More important, chocolate is an allergen to thousands, including some who absolutely adore it.

CERTIFIED RAW MILK   Unpasteurized milk that has been okayed for sale and distribution because the producing cows have passed an inspection for tuberculosis. Certified raw milk must be "scalded" before it can be used in yeast baking.

COLD OVEN   An oven which has not been preheated. Many of the breads in this book are started in a cold oven to allow some rise to occur in the oven warmth just before the yeast is killed.

COOKIE SHEET This is a large flat metal sheet without sides (it may have a low lip at one edge).

CORNET A cone-shaped twist of paper. In Hot Cross Buns, the icing cross is applied to the top of the bun with a small cornet made of Baker's Parchment (see page 234). With a razor or scissors, cut a semicircle with a 9-inch radius out of parchment. Holding the parchment at one end of the semicircle, twist it so that a tight point is formed at the flat end and the round end has a 1- to 1½-inch opening. Spoon the icing into the opening and fold the opening over to close it well. When ready to ice, cut off the very tip of the cornet to make a tiny opening only ⅛ inch across. Hold the tip over the bun, squeeze the bag from the wide end (roll up the wide end of the paper as the icing is used, like a tube of toothpaste), and out comes an ⅛-inch strip of icing.

DOUBLING Rising the doughs of a yeast bread so that the volume increases by 100 percent. Also, in sourdough breads, the increase of the sourdough starter (see page 160). See also Rising in Chapter 1, page 4.

DOUGH HOOK An electric mixer with a superiority complex. A dough hook usually has one hook-shaped mixer and a motor capable of slower and more powerful movement. Nowadays, some of the more expensive kitchen mixers come with a dough hook attachment.

DOUGH SCRAPER Also called a Bowl Scraper. This is a piece of semirigid plastic with at least one curved side that is used to scrape dough out of its bowl and off a kneading board. This is a very handy item, and cheap to buy, but usually only found in kitchen-supply places.

DRIED FRUIT We use only dried fruits in our fruited recipes, not candied fruits. Candied fruits are usually boiled in sugar water— and often dyed, too. Dried fruits are usually just dried, though occasionally some are coated with honey. We avoid dried fruits that have been sulfured.

DROP ROLLS Virtually any recipe in this book can make simple rolls without shaping. With batter breads, spoon out lumps of batter and drop them onto a greased baking sheet or into a greased muffin pan. With kneaded breads, pinch off walnut-sized lumps of dough and place them on a greased sheet, and allow them to rise for about 15 minutes. With quick breads, spoon out a few tablespoonfuls of batter and drop into foil muffin liners (and call them muffins!).

Drop rolls will bake in about half the time of the bread starting in a cold oven, or about a third of the time in a preheated oven. Test for doneness with a toothpick (see page 7).

GLUTEN The protein part of flour, and the potentially elastic part of the dough. Gluten is "developed" (made elastic) by rubbing its particles against one another by kneading by hand, with a dough hook, or by beating, or whirling in a blender or food processor.

GRAHAM FLOUR A synonym for whole wheat flour, from Sylvester Graham, the American minister and "health nut" who, in the nineteenth century, put forward the revolutionary idea that whole wheat flour was healthier than white flour. Thank you, Mr. Graham.

GRANOLA A cereal combining oats and seeds with nuts and dried fruit.

ICING BAG See *Pastry Bag*.

LOAF PAN The pan in which the traditional sandwich-bread-shaped loaf is baked. The complicated part about using loaf pans is that they come in several standard (and a few odd) sizes. We keep an eye out for pans at tag sales and country auctions.

MEAL A coarse grind of a grain. Usually, a meal (cornmeal, rye meal) leaves gritty little bits in the dough—which can make for a pleasant textural contrast.

MISTER A bottle that sprays water in a fine mist. We use a plant mister to wet the surface of several of the unbaked (and baking) breads in this book to develop a harder and crisper crust. It is important that the mister be clean. Even a new one should be rinsed out several times, and a lot of water flushed through the intake tube.

NONSTICK SURFACES Many baking pans and kitchen implements are bonded with a material that keeps cooked food from sticking to them. There are many proprietary brands. The trouble with some is that the surface wears as you use them, and that wear is eaten in the food that comes into contact with the surface. The only nonstick pan we use is one EKCO Baker's Secret muffin pan—we've found its surface to be fairly stable.

PASTRY BRUSH   A brush used in our book for brushing glazes onto loaf surfaces. We do not buy a special pastry brush: We use an ordinary 1½-inch paintbrush with synthetic bristles (that's the cheap kind), washing it well in the dishwasher between usings. We also use it to brush on butter for greasing popover cups.

PASTRY BAG   (Also sold as an icing bag.) This is a canvas or plastic sleeve, wide at one end and quite narrow at the other. A metal tip fits into the narrow end, and icing or any other loose mixture is spooned into the wide end, which is then twisted or folded shut. When the bag is squeezed, the icing comes out through the tip.

PASTRY KNIFE   Also known as a dough blender. A group of sturdy wires held in a semicircle by a handle, used to work butter into flour for pastry. (It does not look like a knife at all.) This inexpensive tool can come in handy working butter into biscuit recipes.

RANCIDITY   When oils spoil, they go rancid. This holds for oils in bottles or oils in foods (nuts and wheat germ are prime examples of foods rich in oils which can go rancid). After they are opened, all containers of oil must be refrigerated. Do not eat foods that smell rancid, they can make you sick. And even if they don't make you sick, they rob vitamins from your body.

RICE POLISH   The outer coat of brown rice, milled off in processing for white rice. Rich in B-vitamins. Use it as you would wheat bran.

RUSSIAN CARAWAY   Also known as dark caraway and burnt caraway, and as *tchernetsa*. This is a strong-flavored seed that has been roasted. It is often used in rye breads.

SCALDING   Raising the temperature of milk to just below boiling and holding it there for a few moments. Scalding kills enzymes antithetical to yeast action. You have to do this if you use "certified raw milk."

STONE GROUND   Most commercial flours are ground from the grain by means of high-speed steel grinding wheels. This generates heat, which is destructive to many vitamins. It also causes a kind of clumping on a macroscopic level. Although stone grinding is a slower and more expensive process, it does not generate as much heat, and makes for a more uniform grind. Both steel and stone grinding wheels wear down as they are used, leaving tiny bits of themselves in the flour. We opt for the stone.

SPONGE A risen yeast batter. A sponge allows the yeast action to develop quite far before a bread gets its full amount of flour mixed and kneaded in; but it must have that flour in order to hold any final rise.

SWEET BUTTER Unsalted butter.

TAN BREAD Any bread made with a mixture of unbleached enriched white flour and whole wheat flour.

TURK'S HEAD MOLD A small mold with a fancy shape and a center post.

UNSATURATED OIL We use corn oil in most of our recipes. It is cheap and widely available, it has no strong flavor to interfere with the taste of a bread, and it is, of course, unsaturated (or polyunsaturated). Sunflower seed oil is also recommended, as is safflower oil (though the latter is a little heavy). We do not recommend using mixed oils, nor hardened shortenings in recipes. (The exception: We use 2 tablespoons of butter in some biscuit recipes.)

UNSULFURED RAISINS Sulfur is added to raisins as a preservative. But sulfur can lead to canker sores if you are sensitive to it. Unsulfured raisins used to be the exclusive province of health food stores, but now many supermarkets carry them routinely (marked "no preservatives").

WEB The pattern of holes you see in a cross section of the bread. A coarser web means bigger air holes. The fineness of the web is often determined by how many rises you give the bread—the more rises, the finer the web.

WOODEN SPOON We often call for a batter to be stirred or beaten with a wooden spoon. This is a matter of mechanics, not chemistry. A stiff batter will often break a plastic spoon and bend a metal spoon. But no sturdy wooden spoon has ever failed us.

ZEST The outer part of the peel of a lemon or orange—the colored part only. It contains the oil that makes the tangy flavor. (The white of the peel contains no flavor, but it does contain bioflavinoids, recommended in conjunction with vitamin C.)

Index

There's an epidemic with 27 million victims. And no visible symptoms.

It's an epidemic of people who can't read.

Believe it or not, 27 million Americans are functionally illiterate, about one adult in five.

The solution to this problem is you... when you join the fight against illiteracy. So call the Coalition for Literacy at toll-free **1-800-228-8813** and volunteer.

Volunteer Against Illiteracy. The only degree you need is a degree of caring.